Praise for *The Energetic Keys to Indigo Kids*

"*The Energetic Keys to Indigo Kids* is an insightful, well-considered approach to raising and mentoring these sensitive, beautiful souls who are our future."

—Sara Wiseman, author of *Your Psychic Child*

"As a father of two young boys, I find Maureen's work incredibly helpful."

—Lawrence Ellyard, author of *Reiki Healer* and coauthor of *The Spirit of Water*

The Energetic Keys to
INDIGO
KIDS

Your Guide to Raising and Resonating
With the New Children

MAUREEN DAWN HEALY

New Page Books
A division of The Career Press, Inc.
Pompton Plains, NJ

THE ENERGETIC KEYS TO INDIGO KIDS
EDITED BY JODI BRANDON
TYPESET BY EILEEN MUNSON
Cover design by Joanna Williams
Printed in the U.S.A.

To order this title, please call toll-free 1-800-CAREER-1 (NJ and Canada: 201-848-0310) to order using VISA or MasterCard, or for further information on books from Career Press.

The Career Press, Inc.
220 West Parkway, Unit 12
Pompton Plains, NJ 07444
www.careerpress.com

Library of Congress Cataloging-in-Publication Data

CIP Data Available Upon Request.

Disclaimer

The contents of this book are not to be used in replacement of medical advice or guidance from your primary care physician. The author is merely sharing her experience and offering her opinion regarding these children. It is the author's and the publisher's intent to make this information available but also urge readers to consult their regular physicians regarding their children's exact symptoms, diagnoses, and situations, especially if they deem a challenge or problem occurring. No warranty, express or implied, is delivered by the author or publisher with respect to the contents of this work.

All of the author's client names have been changed to protect their privacy. Names of celebrities or well-known individuals have not been changed, and this author merely shares her observations regarding those people.

*In loving appreciation of
Margaret Sullivan and
Margaret Sullivan Healy.*

*May your laughter and love live
forever in our hearts.*

Acknowledgments

"Thank you" hardly seems enough to say to my clients. You cheered me on during the writing of this book and let me into your lives. I am so deeply blessed and fortunate to be part of your journey.

Additional thanks goes to Candace Johnson for being a great cheerleader, Jill Marsal for bringing this book to publishers, Trish Sumida for being a true-blue sister, Tess Whitehurst for her encouragement, Pam Durgin for her incredible kindness, Carl Grooms for his generosity, Mary Fox for her extraordinary presence, and everyone at New Page Books for their enthusiasm. Of course, there's also Shiva, who has been with me since 2005 and continues to sleep through the writing of every book—I love that dog.

I am also thankful to countless others from my Reiki students to Agape community members who have shown me nothing but love.

Contents

Introduction

One day in 1979, I stacked up all the picnic tables in the backyard, and decided I was going to jump off of them—just like Wonder Woman. Of course, the problem came when my 7-year-old body landed and my wrist was severely sprained. Ouch! I can still remember the pain and hesitation I felt about telling my dad what happened.

Well, it's clear I didn't understand the difference between TV land and everyday earth reality of physics in second grade. What goes up will come down. What I did know in the depths of my heart is that I wanted to be Wonder Woman, with her bullet-deflecting bracelets, lasso of truth, and special powers saving the day. Something in me knew there was that magical part of me yearning to be expressed.

Indigo energy is like that. It operates often from the imaginative, intuitive, and creative space without regard to "real life" and sometimes even gets misdirected. (See the full definition in Chapter 1.) Looking back on this indigo escapade, I can say that my energy was merely looking for expression. Whether I was making beaded barrettes, learning to play the piano, climbing up the Weeping Willow in the backyard, or literally running away from home, my indigo kid energy needed out.

Over time, I came to figure out how to harness this intensity and use it for good. It's the journey you are on with your indigos. Indigo kids' energy isn't only intense but often highly responsive, sensitive, stubborn, and turbulent at times. They tend to have a deeper sensitivity to what people are saying, yearn to feel fairly treated, and if upset can make everyone feel miserable with their upset.

Said differently, indigo children are learning how to harness their energy and make smarter choices so they don't need to wind up in the emergency room like I did. Moms, dads, teachers, doctors, and healers can also connect with indigos on an energetic level, thus guiding them on how to let go of their intensity differently.

Within the pages of this book, I share how to see your indigos primarily from an energetic perspective and guide you to have more success with them. As you read previously, I understand their energy from a deeply personal place but also professionally. I have been very fortunate to work with sensitive children and indigos, in particular, in the United States, Europe, and Asia, as well as with their parents. What I know for sure is that indigos worldwide need our assistance in learning how to harness their energy for lifelong success.

Energetic Parenting

Everything is energy. This isn't a new insight but something that we keep coming back to, especially as our collective consciousness evolves and expands into something new. I see children navigating their lives through the world of energy. They want to feel good so they play, sing, scream, and shout to let their energy out.

If all things were equal we would do exclusively what felt good to us, too. Tony Robbins discusses this as the pleasure-pain connection. We need to make our goals feel more pleasurable to us so we'll do them. And I certainly understand this idea deeply, whether it's getting my taxes done or meeting a deadline; the idea of *not* doing them is more painful than spending time doing them.

So we as energetic beings are motivated to feel good. This is a positive thing. Within the pages of this book, I help you feel good about raising your indigos from an energetic perspective. My primary focus is to help you understand your indigo children's energy, get them channeling it in healthier ways, and create more harmony in your home or classroom. Because indigos can be extraordinary children if they are taught how to manage their energy and nurture the skills they need to be successful.

The New Children

Years ago, I got a call from *Psychology Today (PT)* to see if I wanted to blog for them. I said, "Yes" and hung up the phone. My next phone call was to my sister, Trish. I asked: "What is this blogging all about?" We laughed. Because I am not a techie like these new children who are born with an innate wisdom to program phones and excel at video games far beyond my Pac-Man training. But I digress.

One *PT* blog that I wrote "The Highly Sensitive Child" began getting hits dramatically and now it exceeds far more than 50,000 hits. So the mainstream world was wondering what to do with their highly sensitive children, and they were calling me at all hours, too. But my love has always been metaphysics, despite my traditional training in child development, psychology, and business.

Complimenting my counseling background I added energy work. It was here that I not only noticed the influx in indigos coming to my office, but the mere fact that energy work and understanding them energetically was the key to more success. Admittedly, I have a great deal of indigo energy and have learned personally (and professionally) how to help harness this energy for greater success. That is what this book is about.

Indigos, Crystals, and More

Whether you are nurturing indigos, crystals, star seeds, or other sensitive children, the ideas in this book can be beneficial. I simply focus on indigo kids because they are the biggest group of children I see being born today that are un-programmable. In other words, they will not just give in and do things the established way. Indigos have a strong energy of defiance, stubbornness, and also sweetness along with their deep sensitivity.

Said differently, my experience is that parents, teachers, doctors, and healers working with indigos need direction on them. They often get misdiagnosed, mislabeled, and viewed as "problem children." Over and over again, I work with adults to help them see their children more clearly versus getting stuck in society's view of these kids as being difficult or challenging. On the most basic level: Different is good.

Our indigos are many things, and different they are. They have a high intuitive intelligence and giftedness where they are patterned for their particular purposes. In Chapter 1, I discuss the differences between highly sensitive children and the indigo personality; I do my best to keep the personality profile clear and discernible.

Quite honestly, I am not a big fan of labels, either. Because so often children (and we) are born not 100 percent one thing or another. We have blends of energies, such as part indigo, part star seed, and part elemental to compose our incarnation—and this is why this book can be helpful to you even if you aren't raising a child who's all indigo. I would imagine there are threads throughout this book that may resonate with you as an adult indigo, light-worker, or interested adult seeking to do your very best with the sensitive children in your life.

How to Use This Book

Use this book as a guide to understanding your new children energetically. They are always reading their worlds energetically and responding in kind every time. As you gain a deeper appreciation for their energies—their energy of new beginnings, genius, compassion, deep sensitivity, excellence, and pure love—you can also help guide them on some of their more challenging energies, too. These include the energies of stubbornness, defiance, impulsiveness, anger, and hyper responsiveness.

Along with nurturing indigos from an energetic perspective, my deeper aim is for them to be more successful here on Planet Earth. They've got all the "right stuff" but need assistance in smoothing out some rough edges, balancing some of their intuitive processes, and developing skills so they can bring their great gifts to earth with more ease. Of course, I want you to be able to connect with them better and create more harmony, too.

So with those principles in mind, the book is divided into three sections:

⊃ **Section I** *(Chapters 1, 2, and 3) shares how indigo energy works.* It provides you a glimpse into the energetic system of indigos, their particular challenges and strengths, and how to help them channel their energy for optimum results. A short energy introduction is shared specific to the indigo energy centers (chakras), their personal energy field (aura), and the meridians (channels).

⊃ **Section II** *(Chapters 4 and 5) reveals how indigo kids heal.* Emphasis is placed on the role of energy healing in facilitating their wellness, and removing issues from their roots versus solely treating them superficially. Chapter 5 serves as a guide to types of energy healing approaches with indigos and is filled with practical tips (for example, crystals, flower essences, sound healing, and Reiki).

⊃ **Section III** *(Chapters 6 and 7) share how to help indigo kids succeed.* The emphasis is placed on lifelong success and how you can be a catalyst for your children's growth. Chapter 7 provides a plethora of ideas for how to help your indigos learn to better protect their energies, direct them, and enhance them for joyful living.

The Energetic Keys to Indigo Kids was created to be read consecutively, meaning that each chapter builds upon the previous one—enlarging ideas, deepening concepts, and answering real-life questions from clients. That said, I am fully aware sometimes one chapter may jump out to you, and I suggest then you go there and read that part because it's immediately helpful.

I want you to be easy about reading this book. To enjoy the journey these pages take you on and be open to seeing things new again. I know from my own life books have changed the way I see things, given me ideas that reframed experiences, helped me overcome challenges, and provided me inspiration when I needed it most. Maybe this book might do a bit of that for you. I hope so.

Section I:
Energy

Indigo Energy

One overcast Los Angeles wintry day, I was invited for breakfast at my friend Sophia's house, and I was delighted to attend. She loves cooking and, frankly, I love eating. It was the perfect match to begin a busy week. The only "catch" was I needed to sample a variety of vegetarian food for her upcoming cookbook. No problem, I thought.

When I arrived at Sophia's townhouse, I knocked softly and her daughter, Daisy, opened the door. Daisy did not look happy and even had tears on her face. In that moment, I knew this breakfast was going to be about more than just food. I entered the house and found Sophia in the kitchen. She said, "Maureen, what am I going to do? Daisy refuses to wear anything but a princess dress to school, and it's pouring outside. I will not let her wear a dress in this weather, catch a cold, and wind up being sick. It's 48 degrees outside, and I just think it's absurd of me to even consider letting her dress up like a princess."

I nodded and said, "Let me talk to Daisy." She said, "Go at it." I went into Daisy's bright pink preschool-aged room, and I smiled. Daisy was wiping the tears from her face, and told me how her mom just didn't understand. Of course, this is the biggest complaint kids say about their parents; they just don't feel they "get" them. So I said, "Help me understand." Daisy said she was a princess and needed to feel like one!

After some more discussion, Daisy and I came up with an alternative plan to help her feel like a princess. She agreed that if she could wear a tiara, and carry her magic wand and princess pocketbook to preschool that day, then leggings would be okay with her. Wow, we negotiated a Plan B that met her mom's wish for her to be warmer and Daisy's need to feel like a princess all before 8 a.m.

Sophia was astonished. She never considered that Daisy would get unhooked, or there was an alternative option. She just shut down when her daughter defied her. But indigo children are often rebellious when triggered and their energy is angry. Within the pages of this book, I share with you how to get your kids from an energetic standpoint and help them navigate their way to greater success—for you, and for them.

Indigo Kids

"Indigos are all already aware they are different."

—Nancy Tappe

Indigos are "highly sensitive with a warrior personality," explained Doreen Virtue, author of *The Care and Feeding of Indigo Children,* in the documentary *The Indigo Evolution.* I wholeheartedly agree. Indigo kids are unique in the fact that they hold two opposing qualities simultaneously: high sensitivity and fierceness. So they are extremely sensitive like the "highly sensitive children," as defined by Elaine Aron in her book, *The Highly Sensitive Child,* but what differentiates them is their personality. I prefer to use the concept of "the indigo personality" to capture their shared characteristics, such as:

- Are highly creative.

- Are extremely energetic.

- Are gifted in certain areas (for example, mathematical genius, poor reading skills).

- Have a need for fairness.

- Prize honesty (almost above all else).

- Feel equal to authority.

- Hate rules.

- Refuse to do certain things.

- Want special treatment.

- Are strong-willed.

- Waver between grandiosity and low self-esteem.

- May be prone to depression.

- Have high sensitivity (sounds, smells, touch, sights).

- Have sharpened intuition.

- Doesn't respond positively to authoritative parenting.

- Have built-in BS detector (immediately know dishonesty).

- Tend to leave things incomplete.

- Cannot be rushed.

- May have fetish (for example, only wants to wear princess dresses).
- Like playing alone (unless with other indigos).
- Get "hooked" on things and can't let go.
- Are independent at times, clingy at other times.
- Seek meaningful friendships.

Understanding the core characteristics of the indigo personality is very empowering. You no longer feel alone. Having worked with thousands of indigos, I can say that these attributes animate themselves differently in children but the indigo short summary is this:

- High sensitivity.
- Giftedness (in one area).
- Incredible creativity.
- Strong energy of defiance.
- Inner motivation.
- Intuitive intelligence (very high!).

When I was told early on that I beat to my own drummer I took it in stride. Now, I realize that I was merely beating to an indigo drum—which is unique, unusual to the mainstream, and deeply powerful as a force for change. Indigos see, feel, and experience life differently than their more mainstream counterparts. They tend to have an unusually high level of creativity, sensitivity, giftedness, and angry energy to channel.

This angry or warrior energy that defines many indigos isn't a bad thing. It is the energy that breaks down broken systems (think: public school systems) and creates better ways of doing things. Of course, the challenge is to raise indigo kids to use their incredibly sensitive, highly responsive, and fierce energy as force for good.

Parenting indigos, especially if you aren't "indigo-like," can be a real challenge. Over the years, I have had countless clients come to me because one parent was indigo-ish and the other thought his or her child was just given to them by Martians. They just didn't get it. Usually it started out like: "What is going on with my child? She's as sweet as pie one moment, and then next it's a full-blown tantrum."

So I usually had parents detail the itty-bitty things of their parent-child interaction, and I served as the bridge to translate from indigo to adult. Then, they'd have an "a-ha" and say, "Oh my—*that's* what was going on." As soon as you know the energetic triggers of indigos you can stop bumping into them unknow-ingly and experiencing such upset all around (more about that in Chapter 2).

Jamal's Journey

One of my first Los Angeles child clients was a 5-year-old named Jamal. His mom, Lisa, contacted me because she discovered Jamal was actually highly sensitive. One instance stood out for her.

Jamal was attending a private kindergarten in Los Angeles, and he was the only African American in his grade. One school project was to bring in a baby photo and post it on the wall, where all the kids got to guess "who's who." Jamal *knew* this wasn't going to work out for him. Jamal is very observant and aware of life, including his ethnicity, and that this was an unfair game. He told his teachers. Mrs. Smith, his main teacher, said she would work on making it fair. So she printed out famous baby photos of African Americans and decided to add them to the game. On the day of this game, all Jamal's peers picked him out first and he got *really* upset. Jamal began crying and left the classroom, refusing to return. He said, "Mom, tell everyone it's not fair and that's why I am so upset."

Jamal was clear from the beginning he disliked this game, felt unheard, and had a sense that it wasn't going to work for him. His teacher, from her "older perspective," couldn't really understand how to create an effective solution. Ultimately, Jamal got triggered by the unfairness of this situation and couldn't contain his emotions. Indigos as a whole cannot ignore their emotions but must learn effective outlets for them. Jamal fits the indigo profile to a "T," with his high sensitivity, strong emotions, and warrior energy standing up for what he saw as an injustice. He refused to go back into that classroom and Lisa picked him up.

Unique to Indigos

Unique to indigos are their mindset and nuanced way of being in the world. Some of these characteristics are minor, and, well, others—they are big ones. I am going to share some of them here, and we'll continue to unwrap them throughout the chapters. I begin with the one that impacted Jamal:

Indigos cannot ignore their emotions.

Indigos cannot suppress their feelings. Other generations and types of children can easily ignore someone's comments, push down their hurt feelings, and learn how to move throughout the world without feeling a thing. This isn't possible for an indigo (exception: if they are medicated). Indigo kids are divinely designed to feel their feelings and let them out. This is where most parents struggle the most. They are unsure of what emotionally is occurring with their children and especially in the early years when crying seems to be an everyday occurrence.

Indigos will always let you know how they feel. They may cry, scream, and talk back to you until they learn better ways of channeling their energy—but one thing is for sure: Your indigo child isn't burying his or her emotions.

One other thing that Jamal highlights for me is this:

Indigos' primary intelligence is intuitive.

Indigos trust themselves. They know when something is right and will stand up for what they believe in time and time again. It's this indigo energy that will change many of our broken systems of government, education, and healthcare, for example, into something better. It's not to say that indigos aren't highly intelligent in the traditional sense, but they do follow their intuitive urges primarily.

Intuitive intelligence is information gained through insight. It is that "feeling" to turn right and then you bump into your best friend. Indigos have a sharpened sense of intuition and reliance upon it. Actually, everyone is intuitive when they are born, but indigos aren't able to easily "shut it off" the way many other people can. It is their primary mode of information gathering and what they trust the most.

Jamal was governed by his intuitive intelligence when he walked out of his classroom. He trusted his inner knowingness. It was this inner wisdom coupled with his need for honesty that upset him so much. Said simply:

Indigos need integrity.

Indigo kids have a built in dishonesty detector. They know if someone isn't honest and cannot bear it. It doesn't matter if the "dishonest party" is their principal or parents; it just simply goes against the grain of who they are. So they stand their ground and "call out" whoever is being dishonest—like what Jamal did regarding that game.

Collectively indigos have come to shift the consciousness on the planet from dishonesty to honesty. They are Truth teachers. Sometimes this means challenging authorities and doing things differently. Jamal just couldn't pretend the game was okay and "fit in" with the other children. He needed to stand up for Truth.

Sensitive Sam

One sunny afternoon in December, I got a call from a distressed dad. Glenn said to me, "I just realized my son, Sam, is a highly sensitive boy. I read your article on *Psychology Today,* and he fits the profile to a T. He also has been bullied in school and is hurt beyond words. Sam's upset not only by his bully, but all his supposed 'friends' that stood by and did nothing. He refuses to return to school and has made the scariest statement to us. Sam said, 'I will kill myself if you take me back to that school,' and that's why I am calling you. What do I do?"

Sam's story isn't a unique one. Over the years, I have gotten countless calls from parents whose children have mentioned suicide. I take every call seriously. With that said, I calmed Glenn down to realize his son was safe and we needed to keep him safe. That was priority number one, as well as getting him proper assistance with his incredibly deep emotions and learning new skills for how to handle them.

Glenn was quiet and realized that his son was safe. I supported his and his wife, Meg's, decision to take Sam out of school. He never fit into his new school and had been struggling socially from the very start. Academically, Sam is actually quite gifted, scoring at a 12th-grade reading level in fifth grade and slightly below grade level in mathematics. This giftedness in one area and deficiency in another is also common among indigos; they are patterned for a unique purpose that isn't represented by traditional schooling systems.

It was fortunate that Glenn and Meg could take Sam out of his school and provide him a personalized educational program. Obviously, this isn't what every family could do, but there are always answers; sometimes we just need to get really creative to surface them. Then I also helped Sam personally as Meg and Sam came to visit me for a three-day intensive program where I taught Sam to:

- Manage his emotions.

- Think differently.

- Speak respectfully.

- Connect healthfully with others.

- Make "smart" choices.

One more complaint that Glenn and Meg had was that Sam sassed them back. Indigos have no problem standing up for themselves, speaking their Truth, and letting their emotions out. As I mentioned earlier: **Indigos must express their emotions.** One of our big roles as parents and guides to indigos is to help them express their emotions (energy in motion) in ways that are skillful versus damaging (more in Chapter 3).

Over the following few months, I continued to provide support to Sam on Skype as he learned how to manage his high sensitivity better. I also helped Meg and Glenn see Sam's perspective on a number of common indigo challenges, such as: *Why does my son play alone most of the time? Do we force him to play baseball? Is a gifted program good for him; he already walks around like royalty? Do we just let him refuse to do certain things? Are we enabling him? Punishment doesn't seem to work; what is going on?*

Spotting an Indigo

Indigos cannot suppress their emotions, they often refuse to do certain things, and they have a unique perception of the world. They want to make a difference and will not tolerate anyone who is coming from the old energy of doubt, limitation, greed, and dishonesty. Many indigo kids in elementary school settings even appear differently because, as I mentioned earlier, they are beating to their own indigo drum:

- ⊃ Poppy, age 13, is a funky dresser with lipstick, earrings, bangles, Madonna-like skirts, and leggings. She just transferred to a new school for eighth grade because her old teacher "spoke meanly to her" and school was boring. Poppy is highly intelligent, although she does get caught not paying attention. (We'll talk more about distraction and how these kids energetically are dialed-into another dimension in Chapter 4.)

- ⊃ Anthony, age 9, is a creative-looking boy with thick glasses (for which he gets teased by kids), an Atari t-shirt, self-made leather necklace, and worn jeans. He loves movies, and has already created storyboards for his first film (think: child prodigy), although Anthony has gotten teased for his thick glasses and unique style.

⊃ Abraham, aged 10, is another indigo kid who is very skinny, has glasses, is extremely creative, and is very interested in fish (it's his fetish). Abe is also scared easily, even at his age, and very sensitive to input from others (how they talk to him, and so forth). When his fifth-grade class (all boys) had his first sex education talk, he left the room and went into the bathroom to throw up. It was just too much for him. (He'll probably look back and laugh someday!)

Of course these are all different examples of indigos who have crossed my path recently, but I wanted to give them more texture and make these ideas come alive for you. Seeing as I have loads of indigo energy I usually don't find them problematic, although they can have many problems if their energy isn't properly channeled. Some common issues are:

⊃ Video game addiction.

⊃ Violence.

⊃ Bullying others.

⊃ Addiction (as they grow).

Understanding that indigo kids have this intense and sensitive energy is a core component to figuring out how to raise them with more ease. I can remember my early childhood and now looking back—holy moly, how did my mom do it? I was defiant and quick to point out the inconsistencies in their parenting approach, as well as jumping in by age 7, counseling my father.

One of the biggest gifts I ever got from my father was when he told me he *knew* that I was a counselor because I was born doing it. As little as I was I could help him feel better, show him the bigger picture (my mom was under considerable stress), and help him do breathing exercises—even in second grade. My mom always told me, "You are an old soul" because I was born counseling.

Indigos are often wise beyond their years. They have access to their inner wisdom, and many don't shut off this connection. It comes out as their intuitive intelligence, too. Perhaps you've had that experience with your indigos where you wonder, *How profound for them to say that. How did they know that? Who told them that?*

Some indigos are even gifted with the ability to predict events, commune with deceased loved ones (spirit realm), and other psychic gifts. Just because children are "spotted" as indigo doesn't mean they have these abilities of telepathy or spirit communication, but many highly sensitive and intuitive kids do. They also have that very real decision to "shut it off" or accept it as a gift like others they have been given.

Whether you adhere to the idea that indigos can be more intuitive or potentially tuned into a multidimensional reality isn't the subject of this book, although I wanted to mention it. I have personally had too many other worldly experiences and miracles in my life to ignore the Truth that there is a very real world beyond our physical eyes.

Energy
"Energy is the essence of life."
—Oprah Winfrey

Years ago, I was interviewed on Blog Talk Radio's "Everything is Energy" program and I had that "a-ha" that everything—absolutely everything—we do with our children is communicated energetically. For example, you might recall a time when you were frustrated (angry energy) and your indigo tuned into your energy as well as served it back tenfold.

Our indigos understand the world energetically and respond in kind every time. They are foremost vibrational beings and connect naturally to the world of energy.

So what exactly is energy? Energy is the power and life force within us. It cannot be seen by most people but is real. Our energetic bodies hold our thoughts, feelings, and experiences that send non-verbal messages to others about what's going on with us in that moment. You probably can recall meeting someone with very "up" energy; he or she was "on top of the world" with good energy. You read that energy. Everyone can do it.

Scientists look at energy slightly differently than us metaphysicians. They look at it as the ability or capacity to perform work. It can be units of energy, like heat, electrical, chemical, and so on. I see the human body as an electrochemical system and doctors do the same. They measure your electrical energy (think: EKG) and brain chemistry (think: brain scan) to find out how units of energy are working in the human system.

Everything is really energy. In my private practice, I work mainly with indigos to overcome obstacles and balance their energies. I perform energy healing sessions called Reiki, an ancient Japanese technique to "tune up" their energetic system. I have been drawn to this practice because it helps unlock stuck energies that have manifested in the lives of indigos as anxiety and depression (among other things).

The Energy Body

You've surmised by now we are not just flesh and bones. We actually have an energy body that regulates our inner energy. Our energy body is inside of the physical body, and also extends many feet outward. The physical body and energy body work together to produce optimum health.

Around the world healers and teachers discuss how vital the energy body is. It is commonly believed that energy moving freely is the cause of health, and disrupted energy leads to physical, emotional, and mental upsets. This is my experience, too—especially with indigo kids.

Subtle energy is called chi in Chinese traditions and prana in Sanskrit (meaning life force). Chi also moves throughout the body in known pathways, and they are:

⊃ **Chakras** (energy centers). These are the energy centers of our body that distribute energy from the universal energy field to specific regions of the body to keep us healthy. Chakra is a Sanskrit term meaning "wheel," and there are seven main chakras or spinning energy wheels within the physical body and extending outward. There are also 21 minor ones.

‍➲ **Meridians** (channels). Meridians are energy lines that run throughout the body and are correlated to specific physical functions. For example, the heart meridian runs up the right arm and around the heart then down the left arm. One symptom of a heart attack (energy blockage) is pain in the arm. From an energy perspective this makes perfect sense, because it is along the heart meridian. The physical body has 20 meridian lines and approximately 400 acupuncture points along those lines.

‍➲ **Aura** (energy field). This is the energy body extending outward from the physical body; it is typically egg shaped. There are seven main layers to this energy field, and they are correlated to the seven main chakras. Clairvoyants can see this energy field naturally and others can learn how to.

When chi is flowing properly it flows to all the vital tissues and organs of the body, supporting their operations. When chi has been disrupted then there can be problems with some of the organs, tissues, and systems of the body. Therefore the proper working of chi in the body is essential to your indigo kids' health.

The Indigo Aura

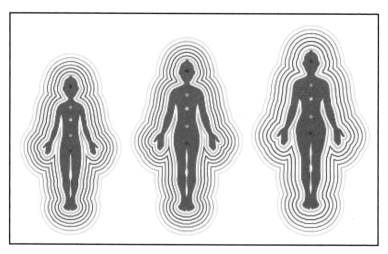

Aura illustration.

Auras surround living things. They are the energetic fields that surround plants, pets, and people among other things. What clairvoyants see naturally is the band of light surrounding those things and specifically our children.

Our indigos actually got the name indigo because the predominant color of their aura is associated with the sixth chakra of intuition. Many parents and children have one primary color in their auric field.

Most importantly, it is helpful to know that:

⊃ Auras can protect children.

⊃ Auras can also contain leaks, holes, and stuck energies (see Chapter 4).

⊃ Indigos' auric health is important.

In this book, I share more information as the nature of the indigo energy system and how to help your indigos protect their aura. The aura can be an energetic shield to negative, harmful, and draining influences, or it can be like a leaking boat. It also filters information for them, and serves as a way for them to attract things into their life like nice friends. We'll work together to make sure your indigo's aura is strong and healthy.

Energy Centers

"Our chakras, as core centers, form
the coordinating network of our
complicated mind/body system."
—Anodea Judith

Energy centers of the indigos, like for all of us, are the chakras. They, however, have different energy and thus operate their chakras slightly differently. As we will shortly learn, they have a tendency to be ungrounded and operate from the higher chakras versus lower ones. I'll come back to this point and help you throughout this book ground their energy better, and help them regulate it and use it to see more earthly success.

We focus on the main seven chakras in this book. The concept of energy and chakras is more complex, though. Chakras are involved in every organ, action, and function of our lives. In this short introduction to these energy centers, I am simplifying them and relating them to our indigo kids.

Refer to the chart on page 47 for the seven main chakras, their locations, metaphysical meanings, and indigo issues associated with each one.

Chakras, when operating in balance, effectively ground your spiritual body on earth. Indigos have certain tendencies to be ungrounded (shut down Chakra 1) and be very impulsive (overactive Chakra 6) as well as let their emotions rule (overactive Chakra 4), which is why we see so many meltdowns. In Chapter 4, I discuss how indigos heal, and we'll come back to the common energetic challenges of the indigos and how to help them operate more in balance.

Chakra	Location	Meaning	Indigo Issue
Chakra 7	Crown of head	Spiritual connection	Daydreaming
Chakra 6	Forehead	Intuition	Trust in self
Chakra 5	Throat	Voice	Self-control (words)
Chakra 4	Chest	Love/ emotions	Emotional upset
Chakra 3	Stomach	Earthly power	Free to be me
Chakra 2	Above pubic bone	Sexuality/ creativity	"Out-of-box" creativity
Chakra 1	Tailbone	Groundedness	Discipline, focus, will, responsibility, trust, safety, fear

As you continue to shift your perspective from primarily focusing on your indigo kids' behavioral and emotional issues to seeing them from an energetic standpoint, everything changes. You open the way for a new understanding of how these wonderful and energetic beings operate in the world and how you can help them (and you!) with more ease.

Human Energy Centers (Chakras)

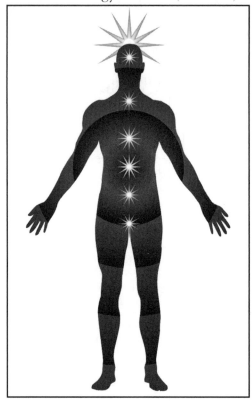

Chakra illustration.

Each chakra has a formal name and color associated with it. They are, from bottom to top: Root Chakra (red), Sacral Chakra (orange), Solar Plexus Chakra (yellow), Heart Chakra (green), Throat Chakra (blue), Brow or Third Eye Chakra (indigo), and Crown Chakra (white). Later in this book, I talk more about these colors and how to use color effectively to help your indigo children.

Indigo Energy

One of my treasured moments was being in the energetic field of His Holiness the 14th Dalai Lama in India. I felt joy and peace in his presence. His energy is calm and mindful in every step. There is nowhere he cannot go without his energy, and if you read any of his books, you can have the wonderful experience of having his words energetically wash over you.

Indigo energy has this seed of this peace. Doreen Virtue said in the documentary *The Indigo Evolution,* "Indigos are answers to our collective prayers for peace." Ushering in peace on our planet, however, doesn't mean indigos hold only peaceful energy but have the unique polarity of being peaceful and pushy. *Pushy* may not be the perfect word, but it's that energy of rebellion, stubbornness, anger, and being a crusader on behalf of our world's evolution.

I am not saying your indigo will save the planet. I am saying that your indigo is part of an interconnection of children who have come here to usher in a "new consciousness" that is a higher vibration of love. It sounds all "woo-woo," but it's not. They (like each of us) are born to give our gifts here and do our best in fulfilling our purpose.

You may be very skeptical now. Because it's hard to reconcile the indigo kid who wants to sleep in your bed every night because of nightmares and that description that I just shared. Maybe your indigo child is an exception, right? I don't think so. But I am not asking you to believe me; just be open to the possibility. Be willing to consider that your indigo may be a fierce bringer of light to this planet—and yes, you have accepted the *big job* of parenting him or her as a dimension of your personal growth.

How it Works

"Even the thought forms you are having are units of mental energy vibrating."

—Michael Bernard Beckwith

Our energetic systems run whether we know it or not. It's like our heartbeat: We don't need to think about it because it just happens. Once I was going through a particularly rough patch in my life and my chest hurt. I was really angry at someone, and my heart chakra (energy center) became imbalanced to the point of some angina. I was in mental, emotional, and physical pain where it manifested in my body.

Children do this type of thing all the time. You probably can see the immediate connections. For example, a child's feelings of powerlessness manifest as stomachaches. Alex doesn't want to go to school and today (like most days) he woke up with another stomachache because his energy is doing its thing.

Every person is running energy, whether they believe it or not. Our bodies are merely conductors of units of energy. Some of the primary units of energy include:

- Mental.
- Emotional.
- Physical.
- Spiritual.

Our bodies are representations of these units of energy. Once, years ago, I attended a class full of healers of every kind, and the teacher had us turn to our neighbor and guess his or her age. I guessed 15 years younger for Brooke. I was really amazed by how good she looked. When we went around the room, the average guess was 14 years younger than the actual age. *Wow.* I understood in this moment that our units of energy (thoughts, feelings, habits) show up in our bodies every time.

So your energy makes you look younger or older, too. You've probably met a 9-year-old who felt like a grown man, and vice versa. It was his energy that holds his predominant thought patterns and manifests in his appearance. (Of course genes predispose you to certain things, but I don't give that a lot of energy because your beliefs always trump your biology.)

Indigo Energy System

Indigos share a common mindset and high level of energy. They are akin to broadband (or the fastest Internet now available) versus many other individuals whose energy is more like a dial-up Internet connection. I realize you know how energetic your indigos are, but I bring this up because it greatly impacts how their energetic systems run.

Indigo energy runs faster and is more sensitive than others' energy. They have all of these energetic triggers (Chapter 2 details them), and when one's been hit they have such fast running, sensitive, and fierce energy often a meltdown occurs. One of my clients, Zach, age 11, is very sensitive. When his mom decided to change the daily schedule, he was quick to say, "Mom, you've lied to me. I can't trust you anymore."

Understanding that indigo kids' energy is so fast and sensitive is a key to having more success with them. For example, Zach perceived his mom to be lying to him, and that was an energetic trigger. With fast-running energy, he quickly got upset and needed to express his emotions, so he accused his mom of lying. Zach is merely doing what he knows will give him relief and letting it out verbally does that. The challenge, of course, is his mother got upset and then spoke to him in an angry way, eliciting more anger from Zach, and the situation got escalated.

The Indigo Energy System

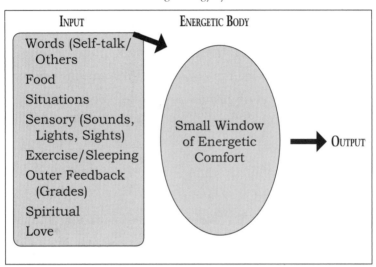

Operating indigo energy.

Suppose his mother realized in that moment that Zach perceived her change of plans as a betrayal and against one of his core values (honesty above all else). Then she could have helped him see the situation differently and channel his energy in a more constructive manner (learn more in Chapter 3) so they both were honored for who they are.

It takes practice to recognize our indigo kids are acting out *only* when they get triggered energetically, and they merely need someone they trust to help them through the emotional overwhelm and frustration they experience.

You likely already know that your indigo kids have a smaller window of comfort. They often feel over-whelmed by sensory input (bright lights, loud noises, strong smells, and so on) or get upset when you remind them about their homework. Indigos are *so* sensitive to the words people say to them, and maybe you said, "Get your homework done!" To them, it felt like being scolded. The tone of voice even can be a trigger to indigos.

Understanding this small window of comfort and helping them widen it (at times) is part of our work so they can operate effectively on planet earth (see Chapter 6). It's not our only work. Sometimes we are called simply to be with our indigos (in their small window) and love them unconditionally so they can create the foundation of all wellness—positive self-esteem and inner confidence to face any of life's challenges with enthusiasm.

Smoother Sailing

"I love my children beyond all reason. They're my joy, even when they're wild with kid energy."

—Christopher Meloni

Indigos are the perfect paradoxical children. They have incredible energy, which can animate easily as love or anger. I remember one indigo, Caleb, who was brought to me because he bit someone in his pre-school. (Ouch!) Truth be told, I see lots of children who have bit someone in the early years out of anger, and Caleb was no different. He told me his teacher forced him to take a nap even against his wishes.

So I acknowledged with Caleb that his teacher not listening to him wasn't okay. He had every right to be angry and upset by her lack of listening to his Truth. Caleb nodded. I also said that "biting isn't the answer" and he agreed. We worked together to let his angry emotions out in new ways and by the end of our first session together, Caleb kissed my cheek and said that he loved me.

Indigos can move quickly between sweetness and insensitivity. They are merely handling their energy the best they know how and responding to the energy being put forth in front of them.

As guides and parents to indigos, we have the opportunity to teach them about their energy, how to create a "sacred pause" between feeling and acting, as well as give them more productive choices regarding how to channel their anger. I share specifics in Chapter 3, where I discuss channeling this energy and offer practical tips that have worked for many indigos especially when they need to get calmer.

Here's some of the other paradoxical indigo behavior that has crossed my path and that I have experienced in my own life:

- Indigos need honesty yet they'll lie to your face (at times).

- Indigos can excel in one subject (English) yet fail another miserably (Math).

- Indigos know their greatness yet many struggle with low self-esteem.

- Indigos are creative geniuses (in one area) but often struggle with school.

- Indigos have great powers of concentration yet are frequently called daydreamers.

- Indigos display high levels of independence when not clinging to you.

- Indigos don't like authority figures yet so often become authorities in their fields themselves.

That was just a short list of some paradoxes that I have experienced with indigos as they grow into their greatness and learn how to harness their energy. One of the things I want to convey now is that I get your frustration. Indigos aren't the "easy kids" to parent—those who just go along with the daily schedule, attend school, and always make friends easily. They have unique gifts, talents, and quirks.

What I have come to understand is that it is in their sensitive nature, high level of intelligence, and strong-willed energy that their gifts are located. They have been patterned by God for a unique role here (like all of us), and it is up to us to help them navigate their way in this not-so-sensitive world.

Next Steps

Your indigos have a preset pattern of energetic triggers that, when touched, can erupt into an emotional storm. Understanding these triggers allows you to do your best to sidestep them, or, when they've mistakenly (or unavoidably) been stepped on, handle them in ways that soothe the situation versus adding fuel to the fire.

In the next chapter, I share the top five triggers of indigos and what you can do to see more success with them (sidestepping the triggers). We continue to deepen our understanding of what it means to nurture indigo kids from an energetic standpoint and help them move throughout this world with more ease.

You might be reading this as an adult indigo, and you'll also find these triggers helpful. I can tell you that these triggers are the triggers throughout life; you don't have them at age 8 and grow out of them by 12. What can change is how you respond to them and what type of meaning you assign them.

Or perhaps you don't see yourself as highly sensitive or an indigo, but instead are solely seeking ways to parent your indigo that feels easier and gets better results. Well, you've also come to the right place. In the pages of this book we keep focusing on not only seeing your indigo kids anew but building our "energetic parenting" muscles so that we can parent from a new place—a place of peace, ease, and understanding.

Energetic Triggers

"I'm an actor who believes we all have triggers to any stage of emotion. It's not always easy to find but it's still there."

—Hugh Jackman

Over the last several months, I've begun hosting monthly teleconference calls for parents raising sensitive kids. After I give my initial talk, I love opening the call to live questions that animate what we've just discussed in a very specific way. Last month, Deb, a mom, asked about her daughter: "My daughter, Tara, is a beautiful and energetic girl. I also don't get what happens with her sometimes. We were having a dinner party and she noticed that someone had taken some of her Halloween candy. I said, 'Sweetie, it's no big deal.' But Tara wasn't having it and decided to explain that her M&M's, Sweetarts, and Skittles were gone. So I replied, 'It's just candy,' and that's when her meltdown ensued. In the middle of the dinner party, she began yelling at me and crying about this. I just don't get it."

Deb was looking at this merely through her adult eyes. It was a few pieces of candy—so what? In her mind, the candy was so inconsequential, especially given the fact that she'd gathered her friends, made dinner for everyone, decorated the house, and set up the playroom so the children could play with lots of great toys.

So I jumped in to share Tara's perspective. I told Deb, "It wasn't just about the candy" and explained that her daughter felt betrayed. It was her candy, and she felt someone stole from her. And her frustration was compounded when she told Deb, her mom, about this situation and she diminished it by saying "no big deal" and let's move on. For Tara, this was a big deal, and Deb's lack of acknowledgment of her experience or help in giving her a wider perspective only incited her.

Tara got triggered. At 6 years old, she did what she always knew how to do, which was cry and scream to let everyone around her know: *This was a big deal, I am upset, I refuse to be brushed aside, and I need to let my emotions out.*

Energetic triggers of indigos like Tara, once known, can either be avoided or handled with more aplomb. Tara's trigger was dishonesty, then coupled with how her mother spoke to her and diminished her feelings. In this chapter, I share the top triggers of indigo kids, what you need to prevent triggering them, and, if triggered, what the best route back to a peaceful solution is.

Energetic Triggers

"People will forget what you said, people will forget what you did, but people will never forget how you made them feel."

—Maya Angelou

Indigos' primary intelligence is intuitive. That means they run their lives initially by how they feel, and if something doesn't feel right, they get triggered. Tara wasn't okay with her mother ignoring her deep feelings of hurt and betrayal. It triggered her angry feelings that rose up quickly and needed to be expressed. Remember: Indigos must express their emotions.

Understanding your indigo kids energetically allows you to also take them less personally. They are merely learning how to run their energy, find appropriate outlets, and make a way in this world where they hope (not sure most of them yet) they can be themselves. With such fast-moving, sensitive, and fierce energy, they are extremely sensitive to:

⊃ How people talk to them.

⊃ Being treated fairly.

⊃ Emotional overwhelm.

Understanding these and the other top triggers (which we'll do shortly) gives you a wider perspective so that you can "see" how your indigos operate energetically. They are always allowing and responding to energy. Of course, the energetic input is introduced to their indigo system, which produces an outcome.

With all this talk about triggers, I also don't want us to overlook the *upside* of indigo energy. It runs faster because it is highly intelligent. Over and over again, I see indigos able to concentrate (on things they love) and produce great contributions. Whether you like him or not, Facebook co-founder Mark Zuckerberg is considered by many to be an indigo and displays those notable traits of genius, intelligence, rebelliousness, and sensitivity.

Embracing your indigos' energy—the upside, and challenges (triggers)—helps you do a very important role for them, which is guide them to their unique greatness.

What Is Getting Triggered?

Indigo kids are actually quite predictable. They are triggered by the same things over and over again. Understanding the indigo mindset is a primary mechanism for "cracking the code" as to why indigos get triggered. There is almost always an indigo mindset-trigger connection. In the chart on page 64, I share the key characteristics of the indigo mindset and common triggers.

Along with these triggers, which we'll discuss with examples and consider the energetic response occurring, there is something else: **Indigos cannot be externally motivated.** You probably have experienced that punishment doesn't work on them. For example, Jane said, "I am going to tell your father when he gets home" and that was supposed to motivate Johnny to clean his room.

Indigo Mindset	Trigger
Prizes honesty (above all)	Perception of dishonesty, lying, cheating, unfairness
Needs creativity	Routine work
Feels special	Treated like everyone else
Equal to others	Any sense of being talked down to
Is deeply feeling	Harsh words, tone, non-verbal messages, and language
Honors sensitivities	Disregard their sensitivities (e.g., bright lights, loud noises)
Seeks meaning	Forced to do something he or she considers meaningless or unimportant (e.g., go to post office)
Commands respect	Someone teasing them
Thinks innovatively	Monotonous work (e.g., boring teacher or subject)
Trusts self	Forced to go against feelings
Sees new ways of doing things	Unappreciated for innovativeness

Indigos can only do things from inner motivation. If Jane had taken a different approach and asked Johnny to consider cleaning his room, and said that she would reward him (make a deal) if he did clean his room, I bet Johnny would have mustered the inner motivation to clean his room, especially if the reward was compelling to him (maybe a half hour of video games, or his favorite food).

So much of our success with indigos includes figuring out how to partner with them, motivate them internally, and guide them toward making smart choices.

Top Triggers

On the path of parenting indigos it is smart to learn what triggers them, how to avoid those triggers (if possible), and what to do when your kids are triggered. Keep in mind that many indigos aren't fully aware of what is triggering them, but they *know* when something feels good and when something is upsetting to them.

As you begin identifying more closely the top triggers of your children, I want to share the top five triggers of the majority of indigo kids. Of course, there are more triggers but these are the most prevalent and pervasive that cut across all cultures, geographies, socioeconomic statuses, and family dynamics.

Trigger #1: Dishonesty

We've talked a lot about how indigos get triggered when they *perceive* life as unfair, someone lying to them, or some system being dishonest. Jamal couldn't stand his school project being unfair and walked out. One of my other clients, Emma, at age 6 threw a complete tantrum because she swore her mother gave her younger sister more Cheerios in her breakfast bowl.

When indigos perceive an injustice or unfair treatment and the adults in their lives don't seek to understand them, they get upset, they want someone to know how they feel, and they need to express their emotions.

Trigger #2: Authoritarian Approach

My parents were really strict and parented in an authoritative fashion. It was "their way or the highway," and that just doesn't work with indigo energy. I responded the way most indigos would, which was by refusing to adhere to their unjust rules. In other words, I had the earliest curfew of all my friends in high school, and I ignored it because it didn't seem fair (energy of defiance). Of course, this approach never really worked out well for me given that I got grounded and had to ride the bus a lot, but what it did do is honor my inner wisdom that sought to "make fair" these really unfair rules.

Parenting that employs more of a partnership approach works best with indigo kids and is what I recommend over and over again. My mom could have solicited my thoughts and checked in with other parents, and we together could have come up with an approach that honored her need to have me home as well as my wish to have some fun. (Ironically, I was such a good kid anyway!)

The bottom line is that any parenting or teaching approach that is demanding and not inspiring is going to backfire and get unpleasant results. So the more you and your indigos come together to create house rules, chores, and reward systems—or the like—you'll be on track for creating more harmony in your home and classroom. Of course, it takes a wee bit more work up-front, but you'll be better off on the back end, experiencing less meltdowns and outbursts.

Trigger #3: Communications

Indigos are highly sensitive children. Highly sensitive children aren't necessarily indigos. It is this highly sensitive nature that is the foundation for indigos and also their mindset that defines them. But this sensitivity of indigos is *highly* sensitive and includes being very responsive to how people speak to them.

One of my child clients, Althea, was 13 when her mother brought her to me. She was labeled as defiant, talking back to her mom and generally not "pulling her weight" in her single-parent home. At the time, I was also Maddy's Sunday school teacher and knew a different side of her as someone incredibly smart, creative, and compassionate toward animals. After working with her and her mom together, I discovered her mom, Barbara, actually spoke to her in ways that were harsh in tone, demanding, and perceived by Maddy as mean.

Indigos are sensitive to the way you speak to them even in tone, language, and energetic feeling conveyed. Barbara was from a different generation that spoke to kids more from an authoritarian mindset, but as I guided her to use softer language, asking not demanding, and generally soliciting Maddy's assistance, things got better.

Trigger #4: Sensory Input (Sensitive, May Be Scared)

Indigos are very sensitive to sensory input such as bright lights, loud noises, pungent odors, and images of violence. They may even develop an irrational fear easily, such as being afraid of people with tattoos. Marcus, one of my preschool-aged clients, did actually develop such a fear. It was affecting his daily life because he would say, "Mom, we can't go to the playground because we might see someone with a tattoo."

Understand that underneath every episode of emotional overwhelm and fear is energy misdirected. Marcus was creating a unit of mental energy that "people with tattoos = scary people," and he wanted to avoid them. His mother, of course, did what she could do to reason with him but to no avail. After several sessions with me, Marcus was able to think about people with tattoos differently and gain some new skills; this is when things improved dramatically.

Trigger #5: Lack of Freedom (Creative, Personal)

Our indigo kids, like us, want to feel free. They want to be able to express their unique talents and greatness every day. Schooling that is the "same old, same old" as when we attended school isn't going to work for them. Indigos need to get inspired, be allowed to see things differently, and express their unique brand of brilliance.

Indigos also tend to come with intelligences that don't fit neatly into a box, yet they are highly intelligent and capable of succeeding. What this means from a very traditional sense is that indigos need someone in their school or educational world to "see" them and usher their gifts forward, versus only seeing them through the eyes of a standardized or end-of-grade test.

Alex, age 10, is one of my child clients. He's in fifth grade and reads at a 12th-grade reading level, but he also flunked science. Indigos are usually uniquely patterned for their purpose, and our role is to help them gain basic life skills (reading, writing, money management) so they can fulfill their divine purpose, whatever that may be. Alex was feeling stuck in school with rigid, boring projects and deeply wished for something more creative. His mom changed him to a program that allowed him to continue with Latin, Spanish, and his other language-related gifts while learning scientific concepts creatively. This freedom to learn in a more open, creative, and expressive way was a perfect match for Alex, and he slept better each night.

Indigos yearn to be free, express their talents, and have their own space to create, create, and create again. When they are constrained by rigid systems they tend to either shut down inwardly or get triggered with outbursts.

The Energy of Triggers

Indigo energy centers are translating words, experiences, and events into blocks of energy that these kids respond to. They have such a strong-willed nature and high sensitivity that often the energy they receive conflicts with what they know to be true. This creates a trigger, and they have a choice (conscious or subconscious) how to respond.

Seeing these triggers from an energetic perspective helps us understand to a deeper degree what's really going on with these kids. The following chart here and on page 72 and 73 explains the energetic roots of indigo triggers.

Trigger	Indigo Truth	Energy Center (When Triggered)
Dishonesty	I came as a bearer of the Truth and to shine my Light into the dark places on this Planet.	I feel unsafe when people lie to me. Who can I trust? Is it safe here? Lower chakra imbalances (1–3, physically focused energy centers)
Authoritarian Approach	I am equal to everyone and believe in honoring that Truth.	I feel angry when people treat me as "less than" them. I feel powerless and upset by being pushed around. Chakra 3 imbalance (power center)

Trigger continued	Indigo Truth continued	Energy Center (When Triggered) continued
Communications	Words matter to me. I feel what you say and digest how you treat me.	I am hurt and upset. I don't think you understand how this feels to me. Chakra 4 imbalance (heart center)
Sensory Overload	I am sensitive and everything impacts me greatly.	I feel overloaded and don't know what to do. *Ahhhh!* Energy field (aura) is overloaded.
Lack of Freedom	I am free to be me. I am intelligent, capable, and ready to express my genius.	I cannot stand doing things in a boring way without any creativity. I feel stuck. Chakras 2 and 3 imbalances (creativity and power center)

Energy center imbalances create discordant energy. This energy needs to be released, and in Chapter 3, I discuss channeling energy. But for now, I want you to know that indigos who experience an imbalance are not unhealthy; they are just experiencing a situation that energetically triggered them and they need to learn how to release it.

Along with these triggers described, I want to share the energy behind two more triggers that keep coming up:

Perfectionism	I am Perfect and want to express that Perfection here.	I feel upset because I know Perfection but I only see imperfection in my drawings, and creative expression. Chakra 4 imbalance (heart center)
Being Rushed	I am at home in the Timeless realm of Spirit.	I am upset because I love doing my things, and then all of a sudden—out of nowhere—I am rushed to finish something or go somewhere. Lower chakra imbalances (1–3) (grounding centers)

Many indigo kids have the tendency toward perfectionism. It's actually not a simple subject but from a metaphysical perspective, it has to do with knowing Perfection, relating to Source (consciously or subconsciously), and believing that things can be perfect here. They came with the intention to help Planet Earth raise its consciousness toward that of Source, which is perfect, and they mistakenly believe they can make everything perfect.

Another way of understanding the energy of Perfectionism is it's the same energy of unconditional Love, Beauty, and Truth. You can teach your little one those are ideals to work toward, and bring more of here—but on this Planet right now it's important to do your best, and release the rest. This is what brings happiness—not the need (desperate need) to be perfect and do everything right.

Also, I know many indigo kids have that *feeling* they are here for a specific purpose, although they may not remember it yet. They were born with the drive to complete it, though—like they are on this Cosmic Mission sent from on-high, and they want to do it perfectly to please their heavenly Father. In other words, this perfectionism runs deep.

Being rushed as a trigger also relates to how they operate most naturally from the higher chakras of intuition, spirituality, and timelessness. They remember within themselves a place that is eternal where time doesn't exist. It is from that knowing that they want to live their lives, and when pushed to get something done on time, or to leave at a particular moment so you are "on time," they become frustrated.

Of course, we need to acknowledge their frustration and help them manage their intense emotions, but with that they need guidance on how they *now* live on a time-based Planet and that we need to work with Father Time. The goal isn't to be perfect all the time but to bring our gifts to this world often within a certain time frame to the best of our ability, and then move forward enjoying our time.

— —

All of the triggers in the previous section animate themselves in different ways depending on your child but being able to "spot them" is the key here. You can begin seeing your indigos' perspective a bit more, and understand how they feel that everything is a big deal and they so deeply want to be seen (partnered with, appreciated, and acknowledged) as well as encouraged to be themselves, which never looks like anyone else. Of course, more triggers likely exist that are unique to your indigo kids, too.

One more common trigger exists that I haven't discussed yet: nutrition. Most indigo kids are highly sensitive to the food and drinks they have. In Chapter 5, I share some basic nutritional ideas that I have seen play into "triggering" indigo meltdowns and how food can be used as tool to balance indigo energy appropriately.

Indigo Energy System

Understanding our indigo kids energetically is a key to parenting with more peace. When they are triggered it simply means their energy has been upset, and they need someone to help them regain their balance.

Our indigos will also stand up for themselves (or others) and often let their feelings known. Most indigo kids aren't wimps, although they have many moments of feeling so deeply that they question themselves, and may develop some self-esteem and confidence issues if not empowered on a daily basis (see my previous book, *Growing Happy Kids*).

So simply, I want you to walk away with these energetic insights into your indigo kids:

- ⊃ Everything is energy.

- ⊃ Indigos are learning to manage their energy.

⊃ Indigo energy is stronger, quicker, and more rebellious.

⊃ Indigos need to channel their energy (see Chapter 3).

⊃ Crying, screaming, saying mean things, hitting siblings, and other inappropriate behaviors are energetic releases.

⊃ Indigos need to learn "more skillful" ways of letting energy out.

⊃ Indigos always match energy (so if you are angry, they'll match it).

⊃ Avoiding indigo triggers is helpful.

Indigos are responding to their world intuitively and energetically. Our aim in this book is to get a glimpse into how indigo energy works and what you can do to help your indigos manage their energy better. Because as you see them as merely "strong energy conductors" we can remove our frustration during a meltdown, just be with them, and when the time is right teach them better ways to let go of their energy.

I also shared energetic triggers because so many parents and adults I meet are energetically triggering their indigos through their speech (unknowingly) and parenting style when partnership in parenting with indigos works so much better.

Avoiding the Triggers

After you have hit a large pothole and gotten a flat tire, you learn to pay better attention while driving and stay alert for bumps in the road (especially in that spot!). The same is true for your indigo kids' energetic triggers. You have probably identified some of the sure-fire meltdown situations, such as teasing them (even if you think it's in good fun) or forcing them to do something when they clearly say they don't want to.

So, like the pothole, it's ideal to avoid your children's triggers. We do this by adapting a new way of being in the world with these kids. We don't force them, we inspire them; we don't to talk down to them, we partner with them; we don't tease them, we empower them; and we don't label them as hypersensitive (or something else) but celebrate their uniqueness. Sometimes this comes real natural to adults, and other times it's merely something people need to learn how to become more proficient in.

Some of the top *energetic keys* to succeeding and avoiding the triggers with indigo kids include the following.

Partnering

One of my clients told me today, "I really wish I spoke to you previously because I found out the hard way partnering works for my son much, much better!" It's the idea of joining forces with your indigo and together creating a solution, whether it has to do with something small like setting the dinner table for guests to something bigger like mowing the front lawn. You don't say, "Go set the dinner table" but rather, "Marc, can you help me and set the dinner table? I would really appreciate it."

Partnering with your indigos work for many reasons: First, it validates that your indigos are smart and you can work together to create solutions. (Remember: A huge trigger is being forced to do something.) Second, it places trust in them and confidence in them that they are capable already. Third, it makes them feel equal to you and sends the message that together you can both learn and grow. (Remember: They need to feel fairly treated, and partnering makes them feel that way.)

Choices

Even a few weeks ago, I heard David Letterman singing the praises of how giving his son, Harry, choices has helped everything go easier. The parent who says it's "my way or the highway" is asking for a meltdown. I am not suggesting that you give a choice about everything; there are certain things expected like brushing your teeth, doing your homework, and changing your underwear. But how you get things done effectively can include choice. For example, Mary can say to her daughter, "Heather, you can either do your homework now, or after dinner—it's your choice. I will need you to get your homework done tonight, though." Heather can reply, "Okay, I will do it after dinner!"

Indigos who feel they have choice in their day are happier kids. Of course, you may be giving choices but really want your kids to pick "Option A," so you can load that choice, and hopefully they go for that one. Although giving choices with children is an empowering approach, I do want to reiterate there are times where choices aren't smart—like "Do you want to sit in the front seat or the back?" for a young child. It's better to follow state law, and that may mean they must sit in the backseat. When choices aren't possible, I usually suggest telling your children the reason they must do what they must do.

Negotiation

Although it may seem counterintuitive to any parenting guide, negotiating with these children is highly effective. They seem to know how to debate, find the loophole in your reasoning, and be able to point out the flaw in your approach to something. But if you come to them and either solicit their help or negotiate, things go better. For example, Eugene needed his son to help him get the house ready for when his wife came home from her weeklong business trip. He negotiated that if Matt helped him, he would make him his favorite dinner of meatballs.

Indigo kids are born negotiators. They seem to intuitively know that life is supposed to be fair and if we exchange one thing (my extra help) for another (my favorite dinner!) it feels like a good deal. Using the tool of negotiation with your indigos kids can be super helpful when you need their help and they want something from you. Of course, I suggest negotiating with smaller things like favorite dinners, a new video game, and maybe extra television time versus something big like a new puppy (that's bribery).

Authenticity

Indigo kids have a built in BS (belief system) detector. Okay, it can be the other BS, too. They know if someone is telling the truth and coming from an honest place, and then can generally relate to them. Most importantly, indigos will refuse (energy of defiance rising) to do something if they suspect that someone is not treating them well (talking down to them) or being dishonest on any level.

Honesty or unfairness is a big trigger. To avoid this trigger is the cultivation of a genuine and authentic approach to nurturing your children. For example, I had a client named Martha whose son, George, knew when Martha was upset. George told me, "I get so angry when my mom is upset and hides it from me. It feels like she is lying and that's when I push her buttons. I just want her to share with me what's going on."

Indigo kids yearn for life to be real, genuine, fair, and honest. They want to have relationships with their parents and friends that are meaningful. Ultimately, indigo kids want to feel safe enough in this world where they share their unique talents and give the gifts they are born to give.

My suggestion is be honest with your kids. I am not saying tell them about your mortgage or other adult situations. What I am saying is to be honest with them about how you are feeling. For example, you might have had a stressful day and your son says, "Dad, can we go kick the soccer ball now?" You might say, "Son, dad needs about 20 minutes to unwind and relax after a stressful day. I can then meet you in the backyard to play. Is that cool?"

By being your most honest self you are giving your children permission to be who they really are and interact with you in a meaningful way. Sometimes (oftentimes) parents mistakenly want to shield their children from their real emotions, but it's in the "real things" where life happens, and your kids will get the message that—throughout everything—you are on their side, and will stand by them in a very real way.

Guidance

One of the biggest gifts we can give our children is a wider perspective. My advice is to explain things to them and provide them guidance. For example, say they aren't allowed to have dessert at 8 p.m. because you *know* the sugar will make them hyper and they'll be jumping on the bed for hours. It's a good idea to not only flatly say "no" to kids but to share your reasoning or perspective. You don't need to agree, but hopefully you can find a place where you can peacefully go on.

Another example is when you are waiting in line. Indigo kids are used to manifesting things instantly and have little to no patience! Of course, this can be incredibly frustrating. One suggestion that really works is: a) Recognize the issue, and b) Guide them. For example, I used to bring my friend's son, Dominic, to Target as a treat to pick out new toys. He loved it but hated the lines. What worked for him was if I said, "Sweetie, I don't like lines either but it's how things operate on Planet Earth."

Indigo kids actually need Planet Earth lessons. They get how to manifest things quickly, but let's teach them about patience, responsibility, life skills, "the golden rule," and provide them instruction on how to interact in this world effectively. (Chapter 6 shares indigo success skills.)

Support

One of the best gifts you can ever give your children is the feeling that you've got their back. I come across many kids who feel their parents are the enemy. School is enemy #2. And some of the other kids in school are enemy #3 (bullies, teasers). No wonder why some highly sensitive kids and indigos struggle with the school experience, and of course overlay the fact that their intelligences aren't necessarily measured in a standard curriculum—they feel like life is against versus for them.

A core quality of indigos succeeding in life, and something that we'll talk more about in later chapters, is helping them feel "at home" and supported here. Albert Einstein said, "The most important decision we make is if we believe we live in a friendly or hostile universe." Helping sensitive kids' see the universe will support them and is friendly to them can make a big difference.

I realize it comes naturally to many of you to be your indigo kids' biggest fans, and others of you are struggling to see their "greatness" in the midst of these daily meltdowns. But it is essential for your children to feel that you are on their side. For example, I had a student whose dad said to him, "Guess you are not Picasso," describing his artistic ability, and after that he didn't want to draw anymore. To him, his dad wasn't on his side.

What I am asking is that you do your best to "see" your indigo kids' gifts, however unusual, strange, and "out of the box" they are. I promise they are there. Think of Mark Zuckerberg, who was technologically gifted. His parents noticed his knack for computers and encouraged him to create programs that they eventually used at home (Zucknet, early IM) and in his father's dental office to announce new patients quietly.

Your indigo may not be a child prodigy like Mark but every child has a particular type of greatness, and if you support their strengths then they'll feel good about themselves, and will develop a level of self-trust and courage to develop them into services (products and so forth) that contribute mightily to this world.

(Caveat: Please don't get lost in thinking your child needs to be good at everything. This is a misperception of our society. Your child has been given a particular set of gifts and patterned to bring something extraordinary to this time-space reality. Of course, there are certain life skills he or she needs, but we'll cover that later.)

The Energy of Partnership

Being able to raise our children energetically and partner with them has a different energetic resonance than "old school" parenting or teaching. It sends messages to our children that we care deeply about their mental, emotional, physical, and spiritual development.

We may be older, but we are not "out of it" and can raise them in alternative ways to help them succeed here. We've also come to this conclusion: Different is good. When I lived in Asheville, North Carolina, there was a popular radio station with that tagline, and it was brilliant because it really spoke to what indigos yearn to feel.

Triggers weaken the chakras and can cause energy imbalances. Using these approaches on page 87 does the exact opposite: They strengthen your indigo children's energetic system for more success.

Approach	What it Says	Energy
Partnership	I value you and know together we can both win.	Strengthens chakra 3 (power center)
Choices	I value your ability to make smart choices and I trust you.	Strengthens upper chakras (intuitive, self-trust centers)
Negotiation	I respect you and see you as a worthy player in the game called life.	Strengthens chakras 2 and 3 (creativity, power centers)
Authenticity	I love you and want us to have a genuine relationship.	Strengthens all chakras and auric field
Guidance (gentle)	I am here to help you on your way to greatness.	Strengthens chakra 4 (Heart Center)
Support	I believe in you. I am on your side and "have your back" no matter what is happening.	Strengthens lower chakras (1–3) (grounding centers)

Indigo Energy Field

One of the keys to helping these children is consistently being there for them and loving them through their emotional meltdowns. Your calm presence (stay as calm as possible) will begin to alleviate the situation and you can—when your indigos are ready—return to logic and help them see better ways of handling their intensity. One mom told me she even uses humor at some points, and her son, Gus, will find some relief that way, too.

With that said, it's also helpful to also get a broader perspective on their personal energy system. Some key points are:

⊃ Chakra imbalances link to Aura Layers.

⊃ Aura Layers are: Physical, Etheric, Emotional, Mental, Astral, Etheric, Celestial, and Causal.

⊃ Triggers are upset energy (aura and chakras).

⊃ Mental triggers come first.

⊃ Emotions are triggers demonstrated.

⊃ Avoiding triggers is skillful.

Of course, we cannot always avoid indigo triggers, but reducing exposure to them is skillful. Our aim isn't also to incessantly manage our children's lives forever either—but to, ultimately, turn over the reins of energy management to them. What this means is as we go along raising our kids, we are also teaching them new ways to let energy out, and channel it into productive purposes (Chapter 3 is about channeling energy).

Changing Our Approach

Oftentimes our children see life so differently than we do that it requires we change our approach to validate their perspective, honor who they are, and see more success. One of my clients, George, is a single dad to indigo Charlie. George is a very traditional father whose parenting style resembles an "old school" approach of telling Charlie what to do, demanding he do things, and then withholding love if he didn't do X, Y, and Z.

Such a tough love approach to parenting may have been effective generations ago, but it is especially ineffective with our indigo kids.

Charlie was also going through a challenging life change, with his mother just having moved across the country, and he felt particularly upset. With this loss, Charlie didn't want to sleep alone and called for his dad every night as he lay in bed. Instead of going in to see Charlie and reassure him everything was "going to be okay," George decided to ignore Charlie's

11-year-old requests and let him cry himself to sleep every night. The problem with that is that it didn't lessen Charlie's upset, but increased it.

George came to me because he needed help and wanted to learn new parenting skills. He said, "My parents just told me things, and I did them." It was clear this approach wasn't working with Charlie, and, in fact, Charlie's grades were beginning to take a downward spiral quickly. So we began quickly moving from:

- Demanding to partnering.
- Withholding love to loving unconditionally.
- Telling to asking.
- Telling to soliciting help.

By changing the way George spoke to Charlie many things changed. Also, focusing on partnering with his son improved things dramatically. George worked with Charlie to make his room a safe space buying him gentle music to play at night, buying frames, hanging photos, getting voice recordings of his mother saying good night, and doing these gentle things to help Charlie feel safe and loved. When Charlie cried out at night, George also went to calm him and help him through this "bump in the road" where he seemed to regress emotionally.

Charlie eventually fell asleep on his own within two months. He also began enjoying life more as he got the rest he needed, and then day-by-day growing into a healthier relationship with his father and everyone around him. Charlie even won the amateur photography contest at his school, which bolstered his sense of outer confidence.

Triggered Anyway

Our indigos get triggered even when we have the best of intentions to "sidestep" that store or experience that we know will cause a meltdown. After all, they go to school and interact with kids their age who sometimes say mean things (trigger) or they see someone behaving badly toward someone else (trigger) or they feel like the teacher is talking down to them (trigger). So what do we do when our kids get triggered, anyway?

We do one of many things. **First,** we let them know we are there for them. If they want to cry, we can hold their hand or help them realize "we aren't going anywhere" but will see them through their emotional upset. Of course, this works sometimes and other times our older indigos want to be completely left alone; they just want to feel their feelings, and get it out. Maybe you can suggest journaling, playing music, exercise, or some other productive outlet.

Second, we want our kids to know that we really are a resource. They can come to us and we will believe them. Many times the teacher says, "Your son never gets picked on at school" but little Joey comes home telling a different story. You need to trust them and help them navigate the situation. Maybe Joey doesn't want you to go to the teacher because the bully will find out, and he'll be picked on even worse. But can you role-play? Give him sample sayings to help him learn to stand up for himself? Or tell him a true story from your life (age appropriate, of course)?

Third, we help them let go of their upsetting emotions in ways that work for them. It may mean crying if they're very young, or perhaps teaching them breathing exercises. The point is that we need to help them navigate their intense, sensitive, and fast-moving emotions—or take them to someone like me who can do it for you—because their energy in motion (emotions) left un-channeled will prevent them from optimal emotional, mental, and social health.

Fourth, we want them to feel completely loved and supported as a sensitive soul. I want you to celebrate your child's sensitivity and begin seeing it as an asset. Because it is in their sensitive nature that they are able to "tune into" what others cannot and deliver to the world new ideas and fresh solutions. Being sensitive in a not-so-sensitive world can be scary, be overwhelming, and feel very depressing if someone doesn't show unconditional love for you as you are.

Being able to do all these things, I realize, takes practice and time. One mom, Pam, came to me about her 8-year-old daughter, Kim. Over the thanksgiving weekend, Pam and her extended family went for a bicycle ride in suburban New Jersey. It was a sunny day and felt unseasonably warm—in other words, it was perfect. Kim was all geared up, like everyone, and was enjoying the ride until she somehow lost control of the bike and hit a tree. She was physically fine but really embarrassed. Kim began to cry. Pam said, "Come on, let's go. You'll be okay."

But Kim didn't feel okay and really wanted someone to understand. Because Pam has cousins who didn't know Kim, she felt compelled to "nudge her along," but that backfired. Eventually, Pam asked everyone to go ahead and then began back at the first suggestion from the previous list—she stayed with Kim, helped soothe her, and promised to stay with her as long as she needed.

Indigos often benefit from having someone older than they are who is also sensitive guide them through emotional upsets, and teach them skills for how to deal with their emotions and begin again.

Coming Up

Understanding the energetic triggers of our indigo children is a core part of helping them manage their energy, see things differently, and eventually learn how to steer their own energetic ships. We are now doing our best to see everything from an energetic perspective, and when these children meltdown, it's merely energy in motion, and they need assistance in learning alternative ways to let that energy out.

In the next chapter, I discuss how vital it is for indigos to channel their energy like Michael Phelps when he began swimming competitively at age 10, or Jimmy Fallon, who took up the guitar at age 13. Indigo energy is always seeking outlets, and giving indigos healthy channels for their intense, stubborn, and potentially explosive energy is essential to their healthy development.

Come along. I promise it will be fun.

Channeling Energy

"I always have more
energy than everyone."

—Daniel, age 9

Indigo energy is intense and potentially explosive. That is why I emphasized understanding the indigo mindset, avoiding the triggers (best as possible), and employing better ways to approach our children thus seeing more success. Of course, there's the likelihood that we'll still see the occasional meltdown, too.

And that's what happened when Kathy called me. Her son, Gus, was 6 years old, and he had intensity, stubbornness, giftedness, and intuitive intelligence like many indigos. Gus also gets stuck on things and wants to beat others in games (in other words, perfectionism). Kathy proceeded to explain to me what happened earlier that day in the park. She said: "Gus wants to be the best. We were in the park and Gus saw one of his friends from soccer. His friend, Mark, actually had his soccer jersey on. Gus then demanded we go home, get his jersey, and come back. I said, 'No,' and he hit me. And then I got really upset, lost it a little, and pushed him into the baby carriage. I know it wasn't the best thing to do but I just couldn't take his anger at me. Luckily then, another little boy fell and cut himself, thus drawing Gus's attention to him and forgetting a little bit about his anger. Soon, I pulled it together and was able to convince Gus that soccer players practice in their regular t-shirts and not team jerseys. It sufficed for now."

Kathy was exhausted. I could hear her frustration at Gus and also how much she simultaneously loves him. In her mind, he's the "problem child" because of his intensity, fierceness, and quick-to-respond nature—not always in a positive way so far. Kathy also realized that she matched his anger and that's when the situation spiraled out of control, thus resulting in her pushing him.

Kathy's story is like so many of our stories. We get frustrated and say something we regret or, worse, do something. But the crux of the solution lies in not only us responding differently but teaching our indigos better ways to handle their frustration, intensity, and angry energy so they can really succeed here.

In this chapter, I share the importance of channeling indigo energy. If Gus had directed his angry energy differently he could have chosen something besides hitting his mother. It really is in helping indigos learn how to harness their energy where they can become more successful in school, home, and even the park.

Channeling Energy

"I have a lot of nervous energy. Work is my best way of channeling that into something productive unless I want to wind up assaulting the postman or gardener."

—Ben Stiller

Usually people fall into one of two categories: 1) those with excess energies, or 2) those with energy deficiencies. If you have a great deal (excess) of energy, you have probably found ways to release that pent-up energy in healthy ways, like exercising weekly. Or if you need more energy, things that add energy are essential to your life, like walking on the beach or eating a very healthy diet.

Indigo kids tend to fall into the first category. They have an excess of energy and—like many of us—these boys and girls need to channel it productively.

Channeling energy isn't a complicated concept. It simply means directing your energy into something else—likely more positive or productive. For example, Ben Stiller realized (at some point), as quoted at the start of this section, that his enormous amount of nervous energy could be harnessed into productive energy for his work. Bravo!

Indigo kids need to accomplish the same type of channeling of energy. Because they naturally have fast-moving, sensitive, and fierce energy the odds of their energy "coming out wrong" is good without a proper channel. For example, Luke, in second grade, gets really frustrated that he has trouble with his math homework and throws a temper tantrum.

Luke's frustration gets the better of him. He hasn't yet learned how to harness his intensity. So part of my work with Luke and coaching his mom was to help them think of his emotions and thoughts energetically. In other words, when Luke got really frustrated, this was merely a build-up of energy that needed to be released. Some of the new ways to channel this energy for Luke became:

- Jumping on a trampoline.
- Hitting a punching bag.
- Building his toy trains.
- Taking deep breaths.
- Playing the piano.

Luke became better at channeling his energy over time. He would tell me how he would use deep breaths at school when he got angry. He said it helped him feel better and mostly gave him a chance to begin again.

Chris's Club

Chris is my neighbor's daughter. She's a delightful fifth grader and also incredibly shy when entering new social situations. One big win we had with her this past year was joining the Yearbook Club, which allowed her to use her incredibly sweet and fast-moving energy for something positive.

Before she began directing her energy into this outlet Chris was feeling down in the dumps. She yearned to make new friends. One day she came to me, and said: "Moe, can you help me? I want to make new friends."

I told her that making friends is merely a skill that anyone can learn and that it doesn't always come naturally. I explained that making friends sometimes takes courage but it's easier if you are doing something you love and can share that interest with a friend. Then the real "a-ha" happened: Chris told me, "I want to join the Yearbook Club," and I encouraged her.

As soon as Chris connected with the yearbook club she made real friends, and her self-confidence began to get a boost, too. Everyone loved her ideas, and she began to organize photos, get captions from classmates, and work with her peers to vote on silliest face, funniest hair, most likely to be famous, and more. Her energy merely needed to be directed into something good versus stuck inside. Plus, it gave her an opportunity to shine doing what she is uniquely patterned for.

Steering Their Energy

Indigos who learn to channel their energy aren't thrown around by their emotional currents endlessly; they are beginning to become captains of their ship. They start steering their energy toward their interests, and also with assistance they learn to let go of challenging emotions in more skillful ways.

Some *energetic keys* to unlocking a deeper understanding of indigo energy include knowing that:

⊃ Indigo energy is always seeking outlets.

⊃ Channeling energy into positive outlets helps kids master themselves (Emotions, Thoughts, and Behavior).

⊃ Without healthy outlets, indigo energy often comes out "wrong" (sideways).

Another way of saying this is: **Indigo energy is always moving and seeking expression.** This energy will come out—skillfully or unskillfully. Indigos who have learned how to channel their intense energy into something positive (skillful) are well positioned for life success. (Of course, there's still more involved, and we cover that in Chapter 6.) Indigo kids who have yet to learn how to channel energy are still letting their intensity out—except for them it's often coming out in unskillful ways (for example, screaming, sassing back, pushing siblings, getting aggressive).

One of the biggest reasons that indigos need to learn how to channel their energy is because their energy is SO sensitive, and SO rebellious. They are vulnerable to become emotionally hurt easily and also respond out of anger quickly, which doesn't serve them. But when you connect a highly sensitive, intuitive, intelligent, and rebellious indigo to an appropriate channel for their energy—world lookout, they can make a mighty difference.

Angelina Jolie, although an adult now, is considered a famous indigo. She has learned how to channel her intense energy for good having served as a Goodwill Ambassador for the United Nations High Commissioner for Refugees (UNHCR) and co-creating humanitarian programs from taking care of AIDS babies in Cambodia to child protection in Haiti. Angelina even commented recently her intense energy was now in check (referring to previous behavior).

Channeling energy consists largely of finding your purpose or passion and pouring your energy into it. This is true for indigo kids. Michael Phelps is commonly considered an indigo and as a child was diagnosed with ADHD. One of the biggest reasons he began swimming was to channel his energy. By age 10, he held the national record for his age group in swimming and found his passion. Today, Michael holds 22 Olympic medals and is currently the most decorated Olympian on record.

Energy Outlets

"Your breath is the bridge that leads you into the vibrational dimension of your being. When things get challenging, stop, slow down and breathe."

—Panache Desai

Indigos who learn how to channel their angry energy in skillful ways are healthier from a mind, body, and spirit perspective. They have figured out how to transform that potentially explosive energy into good. That's not to say they don't make mistakes (remember Michael Phelps getting caught taking bong hits), but overall they are learning how to successfully manage their intense, sensitive, and quick-to-respond energy.

One key to helping indigos succeed in this world is giving them ways to release their emotions and energy in healthy ways.

Some of the more common ways include:

- **Deep breaths.** Your breath is always with you. I find children 2 and older can learn how to direct their breathing and calm themselves. This provides an exit for upsetting energies and brings the energetic body back into balance. After a set amount of breaths, children can feel emotionally more stable. They can also pause before acting. Specific breathing techniques I teach include Breath of Fire and Hot Soup Breath (see Chapter 7).

- **Prayer.** Indigos tend to believe in a higher power, whether it is Jesus, Angels, Spirit, or the Universe, to help them. Given that no one knows if you are praying it is a low-key method for empowering indigos to feel better. At any time, they can silently ask God or the Universe to take their upset and replace it with love.

⊃ **Tapping.** By gently tapping certain "energetic points" on your physical body you can more easily exit energy and come to a place of calm. I find young children do well with the combination of deep breaths and gentle tapping of key locations so they distract their mind long enough to let go of the negative energies. Specific information about Tapping is provided in Chapter 7. (For those scientifically minded, these points are acupressure points and activate the meridian lines thus getting energy moving again.)

⊃ **Creative expression.** Indigos who consistently journal, draw, or release their energies in a creative way are mastering themselves. These boys and girls tend not to like talking about things to others, so often a journal, instrument, project, or helping task helps exit this energy. It may be angry energy that is so intense, or it may be joyful energy that is passing through their system.

⊃ **Crystals.** Sending energy into something like a crystal can be very therapeutic. One of my indigo clients, Mattie, says: "Moe, I hold my crystal at school and when I get angry pour my feelings into it. It really helps." Of course, this crystal needs to be cleared nightly so the next person touching it doesn't "pick up" his anger.

⊃ **Walking.** Being able to move your body and let go of negative energies through movement is really helpful to some indigo kids, too. Of course, there may be some schools where boys and girls can't just get up and take a walk, but many schools now are becoming more accustomed to helping children move and get their energies "out" so they can focus and concentrate better.

Our indigos are conductors of energy, and with guidance they can learn to direct their challenging energies. Seeing as school is such a big factor in indigos' lives, the previously provided exits were given first, and mostly they can be done in the context of school: praying silently, taking deep breaths, Tapping, writing in your notebook, and even going to the bathroom (short walk).

Because the more skilled indigo kids can get at directing their energy, they'll begin to realize their energy is just a force to be used. It doesn't matter if their energy feels optimistic or angry, but harnessing it is what counts. And it's important to consistently learn how to exit negative energies for optimum health, too.

Other exits that are more situational include painting, artwork, playing or listening to music, playing sports, crying, talking, hitting a punching bag, exercising, singing, helping others, building a tree house, and other forms of creative expression.

Comfy Clothing
"Have you seen my Website?"

—Serenity, age 5

Serenity, a 5-year-old client of mine, has enormous energy. She talks non-stop and often gets "in trouble" at school for interrupting and speaking during circle time. Serenity's doing her best to take deep breaths before interrupting, but she says, "School is just so slow," which I completely understand. She's a gifted student, can read already, and just gets so bored during the regular kindergarten-type activities—so for her school is excruciatingly slow.

Her mom, Logan, observed Serenity struggle with managing her incredible energy and feeling comfortable with others. Instead of forcing Serenity to stay at this school, Logan decided to homeschool her one more year, work on a project together (for learning purposes), and then get her into another school that specializes in giftedness.

The good news is this was magic for Serenity. When I saw her next she said, "Moe, have you seen my Website?" And I laughed. It turned out she had created a Website with her mother to sell her custom-designed, personally sewn clothes, pocketbooks, and items online for other children. Her label is "Comfy Clothing," and she's made more than $5,000 in six short months designing socks that feel good, hats that work, and zip-up jackets that feel so soft any indigo would love them.

What I love about this story is it took something potentially problematic (Serenity's intense energy) and channeled it into something good (Comfy Clothing). Serenity's self-confidence also soared, and she wasn't stuck feeling like she didn't fit into school. Logan also took advantage of some extra time with Serenity to better prepare her for first grade, including teaching her breathing exercises, how to take turns, and how to make friends.

Energy Blocks

"When energy healers talk about a
block or an imbalance, we normally
mean a place in the energy body where
the flow of energy is sluggish or not
moving along at the pace it would in a
healthy or unblocked energy body."

—Ann Marie Chiasson

Energy that doesn't get channeled out of your indigo children's energy body causes energy blocks or imbalances. If energy stays blocked for a prolonged period of time, then the likelihood of an emotional, mental, or physical upset increases. Everyone, at one point, has experienced energy blocks. For example, ever have trouble letting something upsetting go and moving on? This is an energy block.

Indigo children are sensitive, too. They absorb what's happening around them (words, feelings, atmosphere, and events) and don't always channel it out of their energetic body. Of course, the result is that their energy slows down and may even cause a blockage. Energy blockages commonly happen from:

- Emotional upsets.

- Physical trauma.

- Loss or abuse.

One indigo client of mine, Grace, is 5 years old. She is super intelligent, creative, capable, and a true joy to be with. Grace also gets "hooked into" things and won't let go. Her latest situation was in kindergarten when a little boy called her "Four Eyes." She kept playing the tape over and over again of this situation in her mind. Grace's energy was stuck.

Stuck energy is when a situation or experience doesn't pass through you—but rather disturbs something in you and gets stuck. It creates a trigger point. As we've learned, indigos already have triggers *in general,* such as dishonesty, unfairness, and unequal treatment, but those triggers are innate to their personality. What we are talking about here are *individualistic* triggers as a result of situations like Grace's teasing episode.

Working with Grace, I helped her begin to see the situation differently and that those kids were being mean to her. It had nothing to do with her and that the Truth was that she was beautiful with her glasses. I knew that we were making progress because she was shedding tears—a true sign of healing, and energy movement. When energy begins getting unstuck the emotional energy connected to the "stuck place" gets dislodged and exits the body (for example, tears are energy leaving the body).

One powerful way to unstick energy is to shift your indigos perception. Sometimes it is easy and other times is seems near impossible. When it feels incredibly challenging, that is where I suggest seeking someone else to assist.

Seeing the Signs

"You have a wellspring of beautiful energy inside of you. When you are open you feel it; when you are closed you don't."

—Michael Singer

Indigos who have blocked energy have imbalances in one (or more) of their chakras, and likely their aura, too. They are in the mode of closing versus opening. In other words, there usually has been a specific event or situation that caused them pain. It is this pain that is stuck in their energetic body and preventing the free flow of energy.

Some signs of blocked energy are:

- Sudden sadness.
- Loss of interest.
- Anxiety.
- Excessive tears.
- Overreacting to situations.

⊃   Change in sleeping or eating.

⊃   Extreme responses.

One of my indigo clients, Julian, had energy blockages. He has a tendency to "take on" everything in his environment as his own—the challenge was that his mother was suffering from chronic pain, and his dad just got laid off from work. Julian's home life was stressful, and he took all of the stresses (and emotional pain) into his energy system without directing it out, or realizing it wasn't his problem.

Julian's stuck energy manifested as depression, and we worked together to shift his mental energy, manage his physical energy better (sleeping, eating, exercising), add healthy outlets, and consciously create energetic boundaries for him. Indigo kids like Julian are very sensitive to their surroundings, and do much better when they are surrounded by positive and uplifting energies.

Removing Blocks

"When energy body blockages are cleared, the end result is always improved energy flow—and sometimes the easement or healing of related disorders. This can involve physical, psychological, or spiritual problems."

—Robert Bruce

Unblocking energy is essential for indigos. They are so sensitive, emotionally vulnerable, highly intelligent, and quick to respond that blocked energy weighs them down. Continuing with blocked energy keeps them playing small and moves them toward mental, emotional, or physical disturbances that hinder their purpose on the planet.

The three keys to unblocking *simple* energy issues are:

1. **Identify block.** The main way to remove an energetic block is to reveal that it's not accurate. It is based on a misperception. For example, Henry was very upset after being teased by his "friends" and decided there was something wrong with him. He thought maybe he was defective or in some way not good enough. The energetic blockage for Henry was how he was thinking about what happened.

2. **Remove block.** Working with my 11-year-old client Henry, I got to present to him evidence that he was actually a great kid. He was capable, worthy, valuable, talented, and perfect in every way just as he is. We also got to speak about the boys who teased him and that they weren't correct. Indigos

like Henry are very trusting and have a tendency to fully believe others even if they are wrong, mean, or somehow not treating them nice. So this is where I stepped in to help Henry see this situation differently—that those bullies were wrong, that he is an awesome kid in every way, and that he can move forward feeling better about himself.

3. **Replace block.** Removing the block was removing Henry's incorrect perception. He then could then see his situation differently and let go of any stuck thoughts as well as energy. I did help him replace those thoughts with more positive ones, too. Of course, there's no magic to this, but daily doses of confidence-building and self-esteem strengthening that must happen. The aim is for Henry's confidence set-point to be raised and his energy to flow easily.

By removing an incorrect thought pattern and the correlated stuck energy things change. The old energy does need to get exited though. When energy has been stuck—especially with our indigos—it may be exited through tears, creative expression, physical movement, or immersing into something they love like playing the piano. (Of course, it can get exited in negative behavior too but we are looking to minimize that.)

Indigo Energy Centers

Understanding indigo energy blockages through the chakra system is most helpful. They provide the easiest way to conceive sluggish energy, which causes physical or emotional upsets. Once energy becomes balanced things improve. Most of us can handle resolving the everyday simple energy issues, like sibling rivalry, failed exams, nightmares, temper tantrums, and the back-to-school blues.

But when energy is continually blocked or imbalanced then our indigo kids often experience physical, emotional, and or mental upsets such as shown in the chart on page 115.

Understanding the indigo energy centers and what occurs from a metaphysical standpoint when a center is blocked is helpful. It allows you to widen your perspective of what health and illness really are. When an indigo is "under the weather" or not behaving well, then there is an energetic imbalance every single time. (Of course, there may also be referred energetic pain, so the heart chakra is imbalanced but pain is in the stomach, for example.)

Indigo Energy Centers	Chakra	Energy Blocks
Connection (connected to All There Is)	7th—above head	Distracted Feel Disconnected Intuition Blocked
Intuition (trusting self, intuitive intelligence)	6th—center of forehead	Headaches (stress) Grinding teeth Nervousness Low self-confidence
Voice (using my unique voice)	5th—throat	Sore throats Earaches Chronic colds Speech difficulty Self-control (words)
Heart (feel self-love, love of others)	4th—center of chest	Depression Anger Low self-esteem Emotional upset Chest colds (bronchitis)
Power (safe to be powerful)	3rd—stomach area	Stomachaches Bowel problems

Creativity/self-expression (safe to be me)	2nd—above pubic bone	Female/male
		  problems
		Urinary tract
		Constipation/
		  diarrhea
		Appendicitis

Grounding (safe to be here)	1st—tail bone	Anxiety Fear Nightmares

Whatever is occurring can be remedied both from an allopathic and naturopathic standpoint leveraging traditional medicine as well as alternative healing. (Chapter 4 discusses energy medicine.) Of course, if your indigo is having a sore throat, by all means, take him to your preferred doctor and get a prescription so he can feel better immediately.

Sharing the energy centers, their correlated blockages, and what happens to the physical body provides a new perspective for healing indigo kids. They flourish when treated from a holistic perspective, and I believe holistic children's medical practices are the future of ensuring that children not only heal from a symptom but eliminate the causes of reoccurring problems, whether they are physical, mental, or emotional in origin.

Preventative Medicine

Providing your indigo kids healthy outlets, and teaching them how to exit their intense energies and channel their frustrations positions them well for optimum health. It sounds simple, but it isn't always easy to step back and say, "Okay, this behavior is just pent-up energy" and then *not* take your daughter's screaming personally.

With time you can begin seeing everything as energy. The checkout line at the supermarket has an energetic resonance to it; you probably glance at the cashiers, and one line is moving quickly because that person's energy is infusing the line. We need to do the same thing with our indigo kids: see them as expressing their incredibly fast, responsive, and rebellious energy in the best way they know how.

Our time is here where we are called to step up, and teach them how to manage their lives from an energetic perspective.

Professional Healers

Many often struggle with deciding when it is time to seek professional assistance. Most calls that I receive come way after the "perfect moment" has occurred to seek help, and now Mom or Dad is finally admitting to themselves, "Houston, we've got a problem." So I want to suggest another way of conceptualizing professional assistance whether it is a counselor, energy healer, or other therapeutic support. Think of it this way: You go to the bank when you need to make a deposit or withdrawal. You go when it's necessary. It's a short-term process to handle what's occurring right then and right there with you. Professional assistance is the same way. You go when you need help with a specific situation and gain the skills you need (or your indigo needs) to persevere and create a happier life.

So the bigger question is: When do you know it's time to seek assistance and you cannot remove the energy block on your own? Go inside and see what answer you get from your inner wisdom. Ask yourself: *Is it time to get more help?* Listen to what you hear, feel, think, or the signs the universe sends you. Perhaps you stand next to an energy healer in the grocery store and you feel a connection.

Another, more linear way to know is to ask this question: Has this situation gone from *superficial* (periodic nightmares) to *serious* (daily nightmares)? Is every day a struggle with sleeping, eating, school work, afterschool activities, and meltdowns? If things have gotten worse or increased in intensity (either acting out or internalizing, like sadness) then it becomes a good idea to consider additional assistance.

Next Up

So we've talked about indigo energy getting blocked, and getting it unblocked in simple ways. In the next chapter, I discuss what is needed to unblock indigo energy when it isn't simple. In other words, I explain how indigos heal energetically and the role of the professional healer in facilitating this process.

Unique about the indigos and probably most fascinating about the next chapter is that indigos don't heal the way other kids do. They take things in more deeply and when they are experiencing deep issues—depression, separation anxiety, and loss—they need a combination of things that we'll discuss to get them back on track.

Because ultimately our role is not only to understand our indigos better and connect with them in more meaningful ways, but to support their overall success. Think of Mark Zuckerberg and Michael Phelps, indigo kids that presented with high energy, unusual gifts, and often hyperactivity, and certainly both didn't fit into the traditional model of learning or education. But instead of seeing them as "strange" or "problem" children, their parents took the time to channel their intense energy, discover their gifts, and move them in the direction of sharing their talents. We can do that, too.

Section II: Healing

How Indigos Heal

Energy Healing

CHAPTER 4

How Indigos Heal

"Healing takes courage, and we all have courage, even if we have to dig a little to find it."

—Tori Amos

Years ago, I had an energy healing session where my Reiki Master saw Archangel Michael show up and say, "Maureen is a healer. Her last name is Healy, which was a sign and her work is with the indigos." It was one of those "a-ha" moments of my life. Certainly, I always had felt like a healer, and with my work counseling children there was clearly a large element of healing occurring.

But when one of the "big guns" shows up and shakes you again onto your life's work you pay attention, and that is what I did. I took out all my books on indigos, read them cover to cover, listened to my inner guidance, and affirmed that now was my time. I had felt the cosmic hand of God on my shoulder saying, "Healy, you are up," so I accepted that call and moved forward focused on teaching, healing, and helping the indigos.

Where it led me has been wonderful. I am now a Reiki Master myself because I discovered that indigos heal the fastest through energy medicine, and when I combine that with counseling—whoa, we see progress. Of course, I also reflected on my own life to realize that I primarily sought the guidance of Intuitive Counselors and Energy Healers versus mainstream medicine.

You see, indigos learn intuitively and heal energetically. As someone with a great deal of indigo energy, I always sought those healers who had honed their intuitive faculty and didn't think hearing guidance (clairaudience) was crazy, but rather honest, and could help me see the big picture when I began feeling lost. (Indigos often feel lost if not connected to their intuitive intelligence and life path.)

In this chapter, I share the five stages of how indigos heal and why indigos benefit from the use of energy medicine. I am not against traditional medicine either, and thankful it was around when my appendix almost burst at age 13 and when my wrist was sprained from a bicycling accident, because I landed in the ER both times. With that said, there is a time for scientific medicine administering to the physical body and also a time for energy medicine for the emotional, mental, and spiritual bodies.

How Indigos Heal

One of the great discoveries of my life is energy medicine. It has changed the way I perceive reality and treat emotional upsets. Admittedly it wasn't a big leap for me, as I have always been into alternative healing, from acupuncture to color therapy, but working with children seeing the results of Reiki firsthand has been profound.

Reiki is an ancient Japanese technique of energy healing. It is used to promote calmness, relaxation, and healing. Along with providing children energy treatments (sessions) I also teach them Reiki so they can use energy medicine on themselves whenever they need it. Dr. Mehmet Oz has even stated, in his assessment of the book *Reiki: A Comprehensive Guide* by Pamela Miles, "Reiki has become a sought-after healing art among patients and mainstream medical professionals."

The use of energy healing has become increasingly popular to hasten recovery, alleviate pain, and promote wellness. But why is it so imperative for our indigo kids? This is really the question at hand. I want to share the main reasons why energy healing helps indigos, and they are:

- Indigos feel things more deeply.
- Indigos don't necessarily have the words for their hurts.
- Clearing deep emotional pain is energetic.

Indigo kids take everything in energetically from the time they are born. They often take in experiences (feelings, thoughts, and memories) that need to be healed that don't have language connected to them. For example, Madeline was spanked with a wooden board when she was 5 years old, but this experience was so jarring to her that she doesn't have words to describe it and can't access it verbally. This is why healing this hurt and helping her feel safe again in the world can be accelerated with energy medicine.

When we are raising children we often say, "Use your words" and want kids to begin exploring how they feel with language. You can say this phrase to indigos ad infinitum and they still cannot use their words on certain issues; they just feel so deeply and don't find the use of words a sufficient medium to express their feelings. This is why so many indigos become artists, musicians, scientists, scholars, leaders, and, yes, even authors because they are doing what they can to bring the eternal (ineffable) into the present moment.

Another way to look at the importance of energy healing for indigos is that it is the medium they are most at home with. It is the language of their soul.

Scared Silly

Antonio, age 6, was my last energy healing client. Lisa, his mom, called me because Antonio was waking up in the middle of the night, running down the hall, and jumping into his parents' bed nightly. He was scared something fierce. Of course, the challenge now was that everyone's sleep in the house was disrupted— Mom got little shut eye, Dad was bumped to the spare bedroom, and little Ava was cranky during the day at eight months old.

The funny part (okay, funny to me) was that Antonio felt great. He got the best sleep of anyone in the house and genuinely felt revitalized for school. Of course, this couldn't go on with everyone else's sleep being shortchanged.

Sitting with Antonio for the first time, we decided to draw. He drew Spiderman and told me how much he loved watching that movie. Of course, I listened and continued completing my own drawing of angels. But seeking to help him, I asked more everyday questions, like: What's your favorite food? Do you have a best friend? What do you think of school? Any ideas why you get scared in the middle of the night? That's when I got a crystal clear response from Antonio. He said: "I am scared of *Frankenweenie* (an animated Disney movie). I saw the trailer and the dog dies and they bring it back to life."

So I asked Antonio, "Is this what you think of when you get up in the middle of the night?" He shook his head YES. As an indigo child, Antonio is very sensitive to input, especially the visuals that he saw. It was haunting, and he had a difficult time getting that image of the dog being electrocuted out of his mind (to bring him back to life). So my first work with Antonio was helping him understand that *Frankenweenie*, the movie, was make-believe.

What really made the difference for him though were energy healing treatments. I worked on opening up his root chakra—the seat of feeling safe and secure. It was closed down, and he was energetically imbalanced. He became very relaxed during this energy session, closed his eyes, and fell asleep on the massage table. Although it doesn't sound like a big deal, for an indigo with sleep problems this was huge.

Afterward, I asked him, "Did this help?" Antonio nodded his head up and down enthusiastically. Because what I did was acknowledge his experience, help him feel safe again, balance his chakras, and guide him to feel strong again. I had no judgment and, quite honestly, I felt a little scared about the *Frankenweenie* trailer myself—so I really got why he was so wigged out and knew that with some insight he could regain his balance.

The Indigo Mentor
"Children must be taught how to think,
not what to think."

—Margaret Mead

Indigo energy and kids need mentors. They need someone to show them the way. I was mentoring Antonio in the last example. What I did was tell him: "You are safe here on Planet Earth. You are protected by angels. Within you is a Power that you can use to feel strong and overcome anything." He needed to hear that.

Kids like Antonio need to be able to trust some-one besides their mom or dad who can guide them along their path. Seeing as indigo energy is so impressionable, they can easily become imbalanced, pick up negative energies (fear), and sabotage their life purpose if they don't learn how to use their incredible energy as a force for good. The antidote to these potential challenges is to connect your indigo with an indigo mentor.

Indigo mentors are ideally older indigos or light-workers who can form an almost instant connection with them. They understand each other intuitively, and the older indigo can help the younger one navigate his or her way—because as we know the energy of indigos is stubborn, rebellious, sweet, compassionate, non-conforming, defiant, intuitive, and brilliant. Indigos see things differently but also must learn how to navigate Planet Earth.

One way to know if you found a good mentor is that both your indigo child and the mentor seem like they are "cut from the same cloth." They don't have to be exact replications of each other but connect on deeper issues. In other words, you've found someone that your indigo kid just likes, and this person (therapist, teacher, coach, friend, or relative) is committed to see your son or daughter succeed using his or her unique gifts.

Some of the common things that indigo mentors help with are making friends, schoolwork, exercise, healthy eating, navigating emotions, enjoying life, and life lessons (from learning how to overcome failures to causing happiness). Of course, it's important that you either pick or organically allow a mentor to emerge that has his or her "stuff together" in many respects so he or she can be a good role model.

Energy Medicine
"Energy medicine is the future of all medicine."

—Dr. Mehmet Oz

Treating our indigos' issues as solely physical means we are treating the symptom versus the cause. Of course, this is essential especially if our little one runs into the house with a deep cut and needs to be rushed to the ER for stitches! Go treat the physical problem and get it handled immediately. But on an energetic level something else needs to be healed, such as: *What caused that accident? Do I feel guilty? Was I not paying attention? Am I safe in this world? Is everyone okay?*

Physical problems in our dense earthly world represent emotional, mental, and energetic issues occurring with indigo energy. When we heal and balance inner energy—things in the outside world heal, too.

Specifically, energy healing helps:

- Balance energy centers.
- Open or regulate chakras (depending on issues).
- Heal aura.
- Zip up auric field.
- Remove stuck energies.
- Clear channels (meridians).
- Balance emotions.
- Ground physical body.
- Hasten physical healing.

Given that indigos' primary way of navigating their world is intuitive, they naturally resonate with energy healing as a way to feel better. I often explain the idea that our energy works in the same way a lamp does: We plug into our energy source, and then let it naturally flow through us. They understand this metaphor, and it's a good lead-in for me to explain that I am trained to bring this healing energy right to them.

Energy Healing

"Although the world is full of suffering,
it is also full of overcoming it."

—Helen Keller

Indigo energy heals the fastest with energy healing. It treats at the level of the cause, and clears problems on an energetic level. Of course, it is not the whole solution—but energy healing is a central part of balancing energies and helping indigo kids feel confident so they can move past any current challenges.

Healing indigo energy also happens in five stages:

- ⊃ **Mental shift.** Changing your thinking can change your life. This is very true for indigo kids and especially seeing as they are quick to feel hurt, make rash decisions, and place a meaning on something that is incorrect. Jacob, at age 9, told me: "My parents just don't listen to me. They hear me but don't care anymore." Having met Jacob's parents I can say they care and Jacob's perception of them was incorrect, and I needed to help him see how they do care for him. This was step one.

- ⊃ **Emotional release.** With hurts there are always emotions tied to them. Releasing of these painful emotions is step two. Jacob also told me, "If mommy and daddy paid attention to my feelings sometimes, and when I am hurt help me more" then it would be better. Jacob let tears fall down his face, and this is an emotional release. Oftentimes emotional exiting means crying but it can also be done through journaling, drawing, exercising, or talking to someone.

⊃ **Energetic balancing.** Here is where the traditional energy medicine occurs to clear blockages, balance chakras, clean the energy body, and protect indigos from any energetic intrusions. Jacob's parents told me, "When Jacob gets hurt—scrapes his knee, skins his hand, stubs his toe, etc.—Jacob really overreacts. So much so that it sounds like someone is trying to hurt him. He cries and screams before he can become calmed down." To help Jacob balance his emotions, I gave him an energy treatment where I balanced his chakras. (Jacob's heart chakra, where emotions are regulated, was oversized; and root chakra, where feeling safe occurs, was completely closed.)

⊃ **Physical seal.** Here is the part where the healer seals the energy body of the indigo and helps bring this balanced energy into the body. After Jacob was able to slowly get up, I taught him about some breathing techniques to regulate his energy and ground his healing in his physical body. In addition,

I encouraged his parents to get him into a mind-body-spirit regimen such as karate or Yoga to provide regular intervals of calming exercise for the physical body.

ↄ **Spiritual/energetic protection.** In the last stage of healing indigo energy, energetic protection is what is needed. So I gave Jacob some visualization exercises (simple ones) that he could use on his own to keep his energy protected and surrounded by the white light of God's love. One of the things Jacob said to me was: "Being Jewish makes me happy" and he even expressed his desire at age 9 to become a rabbi, so I wanted to incorporate his belief system into this. (Chapter 7 shares energetic protection practices.)

The good news is that Jacob is doing great today. I cannot say he doesn't cry and appear to overreact sometimes (in his parents' words), but what I can say is he has gotten into karate, meditates with his dad regularly, has learned how to let out negative feelings with his breath, and also gets monthly energy sessions. His dad, Daniel, also loved my idea of getting him an indigo mentor, so they found him someone at their synagogue.

Indigo Challenges

"Indigos represent the entire range of
human experience, both positive and
negative."

—Nancy Tappe

Indigo kids share similar challenges on an energetic level from depression to distraction. When adults look at these symptoms simply from a physical standpoint, they traditionally seek medical diagnoses and get prescriptions to "fix" their children's issues. The challenge with this approach is it only treats the symptoms and often negatively impacts the child's energy body (depressing it, and disconnecting the child from his intuition).

Seeing as everything is energy, every medication, food morsel, and thought we share with our kids produces an energetic response. And given that indigos are so highly sensitive they often respond in a contraindicated way to meds, or experience negative side effects that made the original problem look smallish. Of course, you can tell I am not for medicating our indigo kids unless there is a serious problem.

One of my new indigo clients, Bradley, at age 9 lost his grandmother. He was coping fairly well with her death and then had a bullying incident at school. Seeing as his grandmother really was his indigo mentor he didn't have anyone at home to talk to, and was sinking into a deep depression. One day he even wrote on his arm: "God please take me. I want to die." Of course, this is every parent's worst nightmare, and a short stint of depression medication was needed to help restart his healthy brain chemicals. This is a good example when medicating an indigo makes perfect sense.

With all that said, I want to share with you my experience with common indigo challenges and how to understand them energetically.

Distraction

Indigo kids are tuned into the cosmic channel and connected to their clairaudience (versus what you are saying). In other words, their distraction is because they are not Earthly focused but other worldly focused. They rely upon their intuitive intelligence first (hearing, feeling, sensing, knowing) and often go to other planes of consciousness to get information, whether they realize it or not and then tune back into planet earth when it serves them.

You've probably had your indigos get reports from their teacher that they are distracted during class, appear hyperactive, or just look like daydreamers, but when you give them something they love—say the video game Minecraft or Skylanders figures—they'll play uninterrupted and completely focused for hours. You see, they leave their physical bodies energetically (astral travel) when they are bored and not if they are doing something they love.

> **Solution:** Energy healing to ground indigo children and also connect them to an indigo mentor who can teach them how to focus (tips and tricks) while honoring their unique gifts. Also, I suggest reviewing their diet, because certain foods disrupt indigo energy, and spark distraction and hyperactivity, especially in our most sensitive children.

Lack of Completion

Indigos as a group have trouble with completing tasks. They even "forget" about handing in their homework (even though it's completed) or following certain rules at school or home. On an energetic level, indigo kids complete things so quickly in their mind that they feel done on that level of consciousness; they don't see the point in finishing on this plane. For example, I was helping my friend's 10-year-old son, Matthew, with his homework. When I asked him, "Are you going to finish this problem?" he simply replied, "I got the answer in my head." And that's such an indigo response! They energetically finish something but need to learn the importance of bringing it into the physical world.

Solution: Energy healing can balance their energy and help indigo children become more grounded. Teachers and parents can also help indigos finish their homework by folding over the paper again, and making it look new. Yes, it's crumply, but they can focus on small tidbits, and it gets them back on track again. Of course, the traditional reward system for completing tasks is helpful especially if the reward is something they pick out (for example, extra screen time or their favorite meal of macaroni and cheese).

Sadness

Indigos either act out their emotions or hold them in. When indigos hold them in their energy is disrupted and sadness may occur. Of course, there is also a biology to depression and sadness but energetically its stuck energy, lack of channeling, poor diet, lack of exercise, and overactive mental energy (poor tapes playing over and over again). For example, I had one indigo tell me: "My mom told me I look chubby and I feel terrible. I just want to hide under my bed forever!" She was hurt and kept playing this comment over and over again in her mind until the energy got stuck.

> **Solution:** Energy healing to remove energetic blockages and sadness, counseling about this situation, indigo mentor to help her cause happiness, an appropriate outlet to channel her intense energy regularly, and also a daily practice that includes affirmations as well as prayer (if she was open to that).

Anxiety

Indigos feel alone in the world if not surrounded by other indigos. They also energetically ingest the energies around them—mom, dad, teachers, neighbors, or strangers who feel anxious, and they "take it on," thus depleting themselves. Sometimes an indigo has a specific type of anxiety (test taking, separation) but usually it is general anxiety or not feeling safe in the world, which needs more grounding and supportive nurturing (food, relaxation).

> **Solution:** Energy healing to balance emotions, clear stress, and ground physical body on Earth. Indigos also need to be taught tools of energetic protection so they are not as vulnerable to absorbing other energies and need to deepen their own practice of relaxation. One

thing I taught my client Oliver was the "happy breath," a type of Yoga breathing where the tongue is behind the front teeth, eyes are closed, and you take four deep breaths to feel calmer. He uses this all the time now!

Fears

Indigos get scared easily. For example, Jimmy at age 5 believed that ghosts could come up through the bathroom drains and get him. He was petrified. I asked if he saw this on television and he said no. Jimmy even stopped going to the bathroom alone, and his mom needed this to get resolved quickly. Her words: "Please help me."

Solution: Energy healing to reduce feelings of fear, increase feelings of safety, balance chakras, and reduce overactive mind. I also served as his indigo mentor, explaining that he was safe, and helping him understand the "spirit world" and how to energetically protect himself. One thing I didn't do was make him wrong; I honored his thoughts, feelings, and experiences while helping him understand he really was safe and that he had nothing to fear. And yes, Jimmy began using the bathroom all by himself again.

Defiance

One of my clients, Hope, said, "I just want to do what I want to do." In other words, indigos are inwardly motivated to excel at things they deem important or they are good at but you cannot coerce them, guilt them, or hang punishments over their head; it just doesn't work. The energy of defiance will be there, and the key is learning how to channel that energy for good, like in exercise, and volunteering together. And when you need something to happen like bedtime, you do need to be firm, and request their help and reward their good cooperation.

> **Solution:** Energy healing to help children become more emotionally balanced and feel a greater sense of calmness. Indigo mentors can also help children learn how to channel their anger and rebelliousness, and use exercise as a healthy weekly outlet. The point is not to eliminate or "work against" the energy of defiance but learn how to help indigos harness their energy for the greater good.

— —

Indigo children's energy is incredibly intelligent, intense, non-conforming, sweet, and sensitive to input around them. With these qualities they are susceptible to energetic imbalances that out-picture in their lives as being distracted, hyperactive, disorganized, hypersensitive, easily upset, unusually angry, and fresh to their parents. Correcting these imbalances is most effectively done on an energetic level, along with proper guidance given to them where they gain new skills, think different thoughts, and skillfully begin to manage challenging emotions.

Healing the Aura

Strengthening and healing the aura is essential to indigo health. They are so sensitive to environments, people, and places, they sometimes pick up others' psychic debris or get drained from the energy of fellow shoppers in the supermarket.

If anyone they encounter "zaps" them energetically they get a hole in their auric field and their energy is literally leaking out. It's akin to a slow leak in a rowboat. And it is for this reason sometimes kids "out of nowhere" meltdown; they've really been slowly and energetically leaking energy and it ultimately gets to a point of exhaustion for them.

I suggest regular energy healing sessions to keep these children energetically strong, and also energy clearing exercises such as:

⊃ **Salt water baths.** Going into the ocean (or putting your feet in) is one of the best ways to clear and strengthen your aura. If that's not possible, you can also draw a nice sea salt bath to cleanse and purify the aura.

⊃ **Sunshine.** Having regular intervals of daily sunshine not only is good vitamin D but strengthens the aura.

⊃ **Crystals.** Amethyst heals holes in the aura and strengthens energetic boundaries for indigo children.

⊃ **Meditation.** Aura Zip exercise is one of the easiest and most effective methods to teach children to protect their energy (refer to Chapter 7).

⊃ **Sage.** Smudging, or the burning of dried sage, clears the aura, and when used with meditation is highly effective to shield the aura from negative energies. (Obviously, this is only done by adults for indigo kids and their space.)

Being able to help your indigos strengthen their aura, repair it energetically, and protect it from energy vampires (those who deplete them) is essential. Because the aura not only can act as a shield to negative energies but it also attracts people, places, and things into their life and of course, we want those to be positive.

Energy protection strategies are shared in Chapter 5 and Chapter 7 so that you can continue to have fun with your indigos as you teach them how to flex and strengthen their energy management muscles.

Energetic Balancing

"Chakras govern the endocrine system, so bringing your chakras into balance brings your hormones, and thus your emotions, into balance as well."

—Donna Eden

Energy balancing is a process of clearing, balancing, and restoring appropriate energies in the body's electro-magnetic field. Our indigos are so sensitive to their energy system running in and around their bodies (chakras, channels, and aura) that if they become imbalanced things don't work optimally for them. They may even get sick.

Some common things that may cause energy imbalances include noise, stress, nutrition, crowds, emotions, insufficient exercise, and negative thinking. Energy healing such as Reiki balances children's energy centers and removes blockages. It, however, isn't the only approach to bring the harmonics of your indigos physical, emotional, mental, and energetic bodies back into balance. Some others include movement, sound healing, and acupuncture.

Balancing energy requires moving any stuck (electro-chemical) energies out and placing positive energies in their place. Over the years, I have experienced the power of singing bowls to place me into a deeper sense of peace and relaxation. Although I never used them for energy balancing purposes, the vibration of sound has the power to heal us and balance our chakras when done by a qualified professional.

Also, I have used acupuncture throughout my life because, like many indigos, I take things in on a deeper level than "regular medicine" can account for. Once during graduate school I was having pain (stress-induced) and the regular doctor said, "You are fine," but I knew something subtle was happening. So, trusting my gut, I went to an acupuncturist and found immediate relief from pain.

Energy balancing is therefore a core component of energy healing and positions indigos to feel their best along with grounding them as spiritual beings on Planet Earth. (In Chapter 5, you'll find additional information as to various energy healing and balancing approaches.)

Tyler's Trouble

Tyler's in third grade and has suffered from anxiety. It began during first grade when he was repeatedly teased by his classmates. He then begged his mom Penny: "Take me out of this school," and she did. For the past two years, Penny has been homeschooling him. The good news is that Tyler is an extraordinary student, excels in Spanish, gets tutored in math, and is technologically gifted like many indigo kids.

Over this past year, Penny adopted a new baby, Justin, and she has been feeling increasingly overwhelmed herself with working part-time, homeschooling Tyler, and raising a new infant in their home. Oh my goodness! The only answer, to her, was to get Tyler back into a regular school, so they began looking at new ones. This is when Tyler began to have bouts of diarrhea and refused to leave the house.

In energetic terms, Tyler's energy system was overwhelmed and could not process his intense feelings and fear. He wasn't nervous; he was nerve-wrecked. Penny took him to his pediatrician and the gastroenterologist, where he had a check-up in his backside, which clearly, from his words, he'll never forget. They wound up cancelling their yearly vacation to the beach, and also missing special family functions because of the long drive; Tyler just wouldn't make it.

That's when they came to me. I worked with Tyler individually, and we did artwork together where we shared our experiences. It became increasingly clear:

Like many indigo kids, he just didn't feel like he fit into this world. Not only did he feel like he was misplaced on this planet (looking for his soul family) but he also didn't feel safe. And that's when I recommended energy healing along with me mentoring him.

Penny had gone the traditional route, so she was now open to energy healing. Working on Tyler I discovered that his lower energy centers were completely closed, and his mental energy was working overtime (worry, fear, anxiety, worst-case scenarios in the future). I balanced his chakras, removed blockages, and then coached him in the traditional sense that he was safe and that maybe—just maybe—regular school could hold something special for him like a new best friend. He was willing to entertain it.

Within two weeks, Tyler was gaining better control over his emotions and thoughts as well as keeping his bathroom issue in better check. They began to leave the house again. I did work with Tyler twice a week for months, though, because our goal was not only to have him manage his sensitivity, emotions, and energy better, but really get mentored. He needed to feel safe and supported in this world, and when indigos don't find that mentor, it can be challenging.

Holistic Healing

"Every situation, properly perceived,
becomes an opportunity to heal."

—*A Course in Miracles*

Energy healing is the fastest way for indigo children to move beyond emotional, mental, and physical obstacles. It, however, is not the complete picture. Along with receiving or learning how to administer self-healing, indigo kids need someone to guide them on their path. So it is the combination of energy healing and guidance that lights their way of greatest success.

In other words, if indigo kids receive only energy healing treatments and think the same thoughts they'll create the same physical (or emotional, mental, or spiritual) problems. There is great value in indigo children learning:

- ◠ Focused thought.
- ◠ Energy management.
- ◠ Sensitivity self-care.

Todd is one of my tween clients, and he's an excellent example. He's very sensitive and takes any self-criticism personally. With that said, he recently got a 60 in mathematics (not his strong subject) and got really depressed. Todd thought his self-worth was tied up in that exam, and I helped him see the situation differently. We are all patterned for our unique purpose, and clearly math isn't Todd's genius but guitar playing is. He already is jamming in a band, has recorded a CD, and opened for a local percussionist. Currently, he's taping himself for youtube.com and hopes to be discovered there.

Working with Todd, I taught him energy healing so he could focus better and calm himself down when he got upset. The real win came when I helped Todd see this situation differently, own his unique gifts, and become more self-confident. It was truly the combination of both energy healing and counseling that shifted Todd's perspective on who he was.

Honing Intuition

Our indigo children naturally tune into their intuitive intelligence and navigate their lives by this faculty. What this means is their intuition doesn't need to be healed but simply honed for life success.

Let me give you an example. In 2009, I was driving up my windy road in Asheville, North Carolina. I typically parked my car in the driveway. On this day, I heard in my ear (clairaudience) something like "Do not park in the driveway," so I decided to follow my intuitive guidance and park in front of my neighbor's house. Yes, this looked weird, but I have developed faith that my guidance never leads me astray.

That night was incredibly windy, stormy, and chilly to the bone. I remember hearing the gusts of winds shake my home's old windows. But I was safely going to sleep, and when I arose there was a loud noise. I went outside and three oak trees had fallen across the street into my driveway (right where my car usually is!). *Wow*—my guidance saved me again. It is this type of self-trust, intuitive intelligence, and navigation that indigos can learn to use in their early lives.

I have seen several indigos use their intuition to help them avoid bullying, make friends, and stay safe. The point is that honed intuition or some psychic abilities are a good thing that can only help indigos especially when balanced with reason.

Intuitive faculties include:

- **Clairaudience.** Hearing one's guidance as if someone (higher self or angels) is whispering in your ear something very specific. Guidance is loving, positive, and helpful; it never asks anyone to do anything negative.

- ⊃ **Clairsentience.** When indigos receive clear information through a feeling. For example, when I shook a former boss's hand, I got the "feeling" she was pregnant. The next day she announced it.

- ⊃ **Claircognizance.** Indigos can just know something. If your indigo has this as a primary faculty, he'll repeatedly just "know" what happens next in the movie. He can't put it into words, but it's a knowing.

- ⊃ **Clairvoyance.** When indigos receive information visually, and it often appears to them like they are seeing their own personal movie (like a dream) before their eyes.

Although psychic abilities aren't the subject of this book, they are real, and oftentimes our indigos are already using their sixth sense (whether we know it or not) to make everyday choices. Understanding your indigos predominant intuitive faculty does help you connect to them and build a strong rapport. For example, if you are raising an indigo who is clairsentient you'll build a strong connection by discussing her feelings. Or perhaps your indigo is highly sensitive to sound; he is likely clairaudient. You see, they hear their guidance this way, so any interference is disruptive to them. Interesting, right?

The Bigger Picture

Over the last hundred years, we've made enormous progress in how fast we can communicate, from Alexander Graham Bell's telephone to the birth of the Internet. Do you remember going to the *Encyclopedia Britannica* to research book reports? Of course, our indigos (rightly so) would think that is archaic seeing as they research, discover, and learn online.

Indigos tend to think technology is the answer to almost every question. They play games online with their friends, read books there, Skype with family members, and teach us about our phones when we don't get it. Our sensitive souls are connected.

Our world has been living at a fifth chakra consciousness of communications, and now we are headed into living at the sixth chakra of intuition. We've made unbelievable breakthroughs with the Internet, social media, handheld texting, and using Facebook as a means to stay connected to friends globally. Our next frontier has to do with these indigo kids as they take the world forward to a place of:

- Intuitive intelligence.
- Energy healing.
- Telepathy.

Indigos are part of nature's way of moving us forward. The bud is always wanting to blossom, the acorn has the oak tree within, and the fetus wants to be a baby. Our new children are patterned to move us forward on the evolutionary scale and bring more healing to this planet like we've never seen before. I am not saying it is all rainbows and smiles, but certainly they hold great potential for shifting our planetary consciousness.

They are leaders, light bearers, energy workers, innovators, scholars, and scientists who will shift how we see things. Similar to the way my father never imagined the invention of the computer when he was growing up, we can likely not even grasp how these kids will change the way life is lived.

One thing I do know for sure, though, is that life will never be the same because of these bold, energetic, and wise children. They will move us from a "me" to a "we" world. And they won't just go along with systems that don't work; indigos will leave their signature on their communities, corporations, and countries so that life is truly better for more people. Of course, there will also be indigos that frankly cause problems because they'll lack mentors, mental health, and healthy outlets, but my intention is to help make them the minority.

The Energetic Key

Indigo children are different, which means they heal differently, too. They benefit greatly from energy medicine and from having an indigo mentor in their lives. It is this holistic healing approach along with other natural cures that resonate deeply with who they are and helps them move forward with greater ease.

In the next chapter, I share a smorgasbord of indigo energy healing approaches that you can use in your home or classroom today. You can pick ones to help your classroom calm down, ease your children's fears, and help them ground more, for example. Along with those I also mention energy healing techniques that need a trained professional like acupuncture, which is so good.

Come along as we explore the world of energy healing for our indigo children like never before.

Energy Healing

"To heal from the
inside out is the key."

—Wynonna Judd

Playgrounds can be wonderful and horrible places at the same time. It always depends on who's watching the children, guiding them, and helping them play well with others. So when one mom, Sharon, called me about an incident her son experienced on the playground, I really wasn't surprised. She told me: "Levi is my 4 1/2-year-old son. He's bright, sweet, and highly sensitive. I am not sure how the other—rougher boys know, but they pick on him. I was helping Levi undress today for a bath, and he said, 'Mom, my penis hurts' and I was startled. He continued to tell me Warren and William put their hands down his pants and pulled his penis on the playground when the teacher wasn't looking."

Unfortunately, this was the beginning of Levi's unraveling. He continued to be picked on at his school by the tougher boys despite Sharon speaking with the principal, teacher, and school psychologist. Levi kept telling his mom, "Please don't take me back to that school" and started crying on the morning ride to school. Sharon was torn about what to do given that she had a newborn, and her husband refused to entertain Levi going to another school.

The "last straw" came when Levi refused to leave the house. He refused to get dressed, put on his shoes, and go to school with the mean kids. When he finally wouldn't cooperate at all, Sharon could see Levi's pain more clearly. She immediately withdrew him from that school and found a new preschool within two weeks. Levi's response was, "Thank you so much, Mommy. I love you and know you worked hard to get me a new school."

With a new school, Levi stopped the morning tears, although had other challenges. He was increasingly scared, afraid to make new friends, started getting night-mares, became more defiant at home, and tuned out his parents. Sharon said, "Levi used to be so outgoing and now he hides behind me when meeting new people." And this is when she brought him to me for help.

Over many months, I worked with Levi to help him feel safe again, make new friends, and manage his energy better. He understandably was shaken and with weekly energy healing sessions he improved dra-matically. I also served as his indigo mentor working with him on very specific tactics to make friends, let go of the past, sleep better, and heal.

In this chapter, I share some of the techniques that I used with Levi, like energy healing, Tapping, and the use of crystals to help him heal. Along with those I share others so you can pick and choose what makes the most sense for you and your indigo children. I love all of these different healing methods and hope you find an absolute gem in here for you, too.

Energy Healing

"Energy can be moved in the energy body through movement, touch, sound and vibration, the breath, electricity or current, light, and magnets."

—Ann Marie Chiasson, MD

Our energy body is a light body. It literally is composed of light, sound, vibration, and electrical impulses moving energy. So when we heal the energy body, we get to look at a wide variety of methodologies that can shift the resonance of this body (aura, meridian, chakras) and bring it back into balance.

Energy that has been stuck or sluggish begins moving again. There are no longer major chakra imbalances, either. Energy centers with "too much" energy lessen, and those that are closed or depleted get filled up. Personal energy fields get stronger and with focused intention become protected against lower energies.

Healing the energy body is also intimately connected to the physical body's health. One cannot change without changing the other. Improving one's energetic health also helps radically shift one's emotional, mental, and spiritual outlook. Soon there becomes more energy and vitality to do the things one wants to do.

Indigo children are drawn to energy healing, too. They love the types of things that lift up their energy and help them feel good. Some of the energy healing methods that I use with indigos repeatedly include:

ↄ Hands-on healing (Reiki).

ↄ Crystals.

⊃ Flower essences.

⊃ Color.

⊃ Sound.

In this chapter, I explore these energy healing methods and how you can use them with your indigos. Specific issues such as how to ground your indigos, help soothe their worries, calm their fears, and help them over emotional upsets are addressed. Along with these energetic tools I also consider nutrition, nature, movement, meditation, and more.

Seeing as indigo children are all different it's always a matter of finding what works well for your children, how to ease their upsets, strengthen them inside, and move them forward with more confidence that they can be who they came here to be. Of course, in this process of supporting our strong-willed children, we are also creating more harmony at home and connecting with them in better ways.

Hands-On Healing

"Whatever house I enter I shall come to heal."

—Hippocratic Oath

Choosing to become an energy healer was the next logical step for me. Having worked with indigo children for years, seeing them "stay stuck" in certain issues and then discovering that through the use of energy work they became unstuck quicker, it really was a no-brainer for me to incorporate energy healing into my work.

Of all the energy healing methods, I feel like Reiki chose me for a number of reasons. It is Eastern in origin (similar to my training), has a clear lineage, and is the most reputable worldwide in the field of energy medicine. I was particularly sensitive to how it was perceived, given that my work is with providing energy healing to children and teaching them how to heal themselves.

Reiki roughly means universal life energy. The "Rei" means universal or infinite intelligence, and the "Ki" is similar to "chi" in Chinese, meaning energy. One question I often get is: *Is Reiki a spiritual experience?* And I believe everything is a spiritual experience (even pooping) but certainly I use the Reiki energy reverentially and treat sessions as a place to heal. My only suggestion is that children be open to receiving healing energy.

What really happens when I bring my indigo children for a Reiki healing session? Well, I can go into great detail, but let me give you the highlights:

   ꙩ   Indigos lay on a massage table (typically).

- Light touch is commonplace (head, shoulders, arms, stomach, legs, feet).

- Reiki practitioners can also beam energy (no touch needed).

- Sessions last from 15 to 45 minutes depending on age.

- Energy centers are the focus.

- Auric health is improved.

- Meridians open.

Oftentimes I have indigos fall asleep on the massage table. They are brought to me usually for something very specific—like Levi's issue of having been bullied or Antonio's (from Chapter 4) issue of having reoccurring nightmares. Because calming their system, grounding them, clearing blocks, and then repairing whatever needs to occur in their energetic system creates a greater sense of ease.

With more ease and calmness indigo children are then open to learn new skills and ways of being in the world that work better for them. After a Reiki session, Levi was certainly able to relax more, listen better, and begin to let the past go. I explained to him that he is powerful, and by talking about those bullies over and over again, he was giving them his power, and he could be using that energy to be having more fun now. He got it. (We also chatted about forgiveness as a key to our own happiness, which he was really considering.)

Crystals

"Crystals have been used for millennia
to heal and bring balance."

—Judy Hall

Crystals are central to many cultures globally. They are considered to have protective, healing, and powerful qualities. Children growing up within cultures from Mexico, Tibet, Peru, Persia, Native America, and more wear amulets from the start. It is because crystals can conduct, protect, and transmute energies.

Within today's modern world, crystals are commonly used in computers, clocks, televisions, radios, and other communication devices. They can amplify sound, transmit light waves, and transfer energy. Although we don't commonly discuss the many mainstream uses of crystals, they are everywhere.

Using crystals as healing agents began thousands of years ago. Ancient Egyptians laid crystals on certain locations to add energy and to remove toxins from wounds. They also created elixirs to reduce nightmares and cure insomnia. Native American Indians also connected with crystals deeply using them in their baptismal rituals (seven stones in running water) and to protect their children on their sacred journey.

So using crystals for therapeutic and medicinal purposes isn't new. What is new is the rise in popularity and increasing acceptance from parents and teachers that:

⊃ Crystals conduct energy.

⊃ Children are influenced by crystals.

⊃ Crystal therapy is real.

Over the last 10 years, I have noticed a steady increase in the number of parents who inquire about crystal prescriptions. They've heard me mention using crystals to calm their children and help them sleep or something very specific. Gone are the days when using gemstones for healing purposes needed to be spoken about quietly; we have now entered the age of Pisces (spirituality and intuition).

Amelia's Anger

One of my indigo students, Amelia, loves using crystals. She attended one of my Reiki One classes where I attuned her to the Reiki energy. Seeing as her class was also full of indigos and they all were incredibly interested in crystals, we talked about how to use Reiki to feel calmer and more relaxed, and how gemstones can also help.

Specifically, Amelia shared with the group: "Sometimes I get so angry! My sister borrows my clothes without asking, and yesterday she broke my headset. I just want to scream. So what I've been doing to help me is picking a stone from my room, holding it, and putting all my anger into it. I totally feel the anger going into the stone."

At age 11, Amelia is doing pretty well to realize how to channel her indigo energy, let her emotions out, and use crystals. Sometimes she would use a clear Quartz (programmable stone), and other times Rose Quartz. Of course, it is important to clear the quartz of her anger before she used it again or shared it with anyone.

Note: Reiki is a taught and caught teaching. It needs to be taught by a qualified instructor, and it's also caught (passed down non-verbally through an attunement) in person by your teacher.

Crystal Healing
"Crystals are powerful healing tools, and you can use them to boost your natural spiritual healing power."

—Doreen Virtue and Judith Lukomski

Crystals have electromagnetic fields, and when they come into contact with indigo children they can influence their personal energy field (aura) and inner energy (chakras and meridians). So using crystals skillfully is important—it's not "woo-woo" at all but deeply scientific and, as mentioned, historically significant.

Certain crystals can open energy channels, repair and protect the auric field, create calmness, ease tension, balance chakras, and soothe upsets. Indigo children intuitively sense this power of crystals and resonate so deeply with them. Some of the practical ways you can use crystals include:

- **Grids.** Crystals placed in a certain geometric pattern (sacred shape) create a vortex of healing energy to be used for a particular purpose. One well-known energetic grid is Stonehenge in England. With regard to our indigos, I often find myself recommending that parents create a grid of selenite (four pieces for each corner) in the bedroom to reduce nighttime fears, and promote relaxation and better sleep.

- **Protection.** Wearing, carrying, or holding gemstones can offer protection from lower and negative energies. Given that indigos are so sensitive it's important to find a stone that feels good to them, and also offers energy protection (against energy drains and attacks). I love wearing Amethyst, Moonstone, Aquamarine, or Tigers Eye for protection. Other stones that can work well for protection include: Lapis Lazuli, Fluorite, Blue Agate, and Turquoise.

⊃ **Grounding.** Oftentimes indigos find themselves ungrounded and that means they need to strengthen their connection to Planet Earth (using lower chakras). Carnelian (color of base chakra), Tigers Eye (gentle stone), Hematite, and Obsidian are solid grounding stones. But I suggest taking your indigo to the store and seeing what he is guided to, then looking it up and seeing if it fits the issue perfectly (often it does).

⊃ **Healing.** Crystals placed on energy centers (or near them) can have a powerful impact on balancing energies. Along with the seven major energy centers, the 21 minor ones can be used, too (for example, hands and feet). Along with the ancient art of gemstone placement, some healers create elixirs (non-alcoholic) today that are believed to contain healing properties, too.

Using crystals has become part of my healing practice. I find that indigos and other sensitive children respond immediately to the energy. And if used in combination with Reiki, acupuncture, flower essences, or other energy healing therapies, I find them increasingly effective. One more way to use crystals is to infuse them with positive energy, and then give them to your indigos so they can access that strength whenever they need it.

One of my teachers, Starr, is an energy worker (although I didn't learn that from her) and gave me a self-healed crystal. It sits on my desk in a position of honor. She had programmed it and gave it to me the week after my mother died. Over the years, I have held it close to my heart and appreciated the courageous energy she has poured into it for me.

Crystals by Chakra

Indigo energy centers (chakras) hold energy for a particular purpose, and when they are operating in balance your children can be successful here. Oftentimes our indigos, however, are operating with energetic detours in their system; they have under-performing lower chakras (ungrounded) and over-performing high chakras (intuition, creativity, innovation), leaving them ineffectual here.

Energy Center	Color	Short Meaning	Stone	Helps With
Crown	White	Spiritual Connection	Tibetan Quartz, Fishtail Selenite, Celesite	Love, trust in God, clarity
Third Eye	Indigo	Intuition	Amethyst, Moonstone, Purple Fluorite, Blue Topaz	Intuition, self-trust
Throat	Blue	Communication	Lapis Lazuli, Turquoise, Blue Lace Agate, Aquamarine, Larimar, Celesite	Speaking up, impulse control
Heart	Green	Love	Rose Quartz, Jade, Peridot, Green Aventurine, Green Calcite	Emotional balance
Solar Plexus	Yellow	Power	Citrine, Yellow Tourmaline	Inner strength
Sacral	Orange	Creativity	Orange Carnelian, Orange Calcite, Red Jasper	Self-expression, creative energy
Root	Red	Survival	Carnelian, Black Obsidian, Black Tourmaline, Amber, Labradorite	Grounding

Note: The chart is provided as a starting point.

One way of helping balance indigo energy relatively easily and effectively is to lay gemstones near energy centers. Given that crystals work through vibration, these precious stones will either lower or raise the vibration of an energy center, thus bringing it back into balance. It is a concept held commonly in Eastern medicine.

Indigo energy centers are more like signatures, with every child having a unique blending of colors in each locale. I often see the heart chakra with green and pink, not just green, and also indigo children that have indigo everywhere. By balancing indigo energies (colors, vibrations) in each chakra, these children can operate more effectively on Planet Earth and actually do what they came here to do.

One of my indigo clients, Lily, age 12, is a straight-A student. She is so very bright, and when I met her she had indigo everywhere. Her root chakra wasn't red (no grounding) and she was forgetting to do things. For example, Lily would complete her homework (100 percent correct) but forget to turn it in. Ultimately, she was done "in her mind," but she needed to ground her energy and be a success here on Planet Earth, too.

Working with Lily, I found her extremely responsive to Reiki and also the use of crystals during our sessions. Along with balancing her energies, I also worked with her to create crystal prescriptions for better grounding, aura protection, and task completion. She picked a Carnelian and Lapis Lazuli combination for grounding, which immediately strengthened her connection to Mother Earth.

Aura Stones

Aura Protection	Malachite Moonstone Amethyst Labradorite
Aura Repair	Green Fluorite Mahogany Obsidian Red Jasper

Choosing a stone that has strong protective properties along with teaching indigos how to visually see themselves surrounded with light (bubble of light), or closing off their personal energy field (Aura Zip in Chapter 7), helps energetically protect them. They learn how to create strong energetic boundaries, and if needed they can continually shield themselves from negative energies throughout the day (ask for angelic assistance, for example).

Indigo Cures

Energy Issue	Indigo Cure
Reduce hyperactivity	Lapis Lazuli
Release energy	Moonstone
Calming	Aquamarine
Release stuck emotions	Rose Quartz
Encourage balance and calmness	Blue Topaz, Green Aventurine
Grounding	Obsidian, Fluorite, Tigers Eye, Carnelian

Some additional books that may be of interest to you are *Crystal Prescriptions* by Judy Hall and *The Healing Crystals First Aid Manual* by Michael Gienger.

Flower Healing

"They...cure by flooding our bodies with the beautiful vibrations of our Higher Nature, in the presence of which, disease melts away as snow in the sunshine."

—Dr. Edward Bach, founder of Bach Flower Remedies

Stopping to smell the flowers is more than just an idiom. Sure, it can relax your system, but there is the potential to feel more energized, balanced, and healthier, too. It is the appearance, fragrance, essence, energy, and life force of the flowers that can calm your indigo children's upsets and soothe their soul.

Similar to the idea that crystals interact with our children's personal energy field, so does the essence or energy of flowers. Every type of flower also has a different energy and healing quality to it. Some may hype your children up, whereas others will certainly guide them to feel more relaxed at bedtime.

Using real flowers, creating (or buying) your own essences, sprays, baths, or finding original ways to connect with flowers can be fun. They can teach us how this planet has the power to provide for us in very powerful ways. It reminds me of the Native American belief that if you were wounded, the cure would be somewhere around you. In other words, the flowers that surround us can help us.

Earlier today, I stepped outside to discover the very first roses blooming of this new spring season. They are pink and white. Years ago, I also attended a class about the power of roses, and they are commonly considered to hold the highest vibration (most pure essence). It is interesting to me that roses are used at the Vatican in making rosary beads—they symbolically hold the energy of purity and love—and

Edgar Cayce, the popular mystic, also suggested the power of rose water for clearing spaces.

Connecting with the power of flowers isn't a new, 21st-century event; however, using flower essences (baths, sprays, or fresh flowers) as an energetic key to calming, strengthening, and empowering our indigos may be.

Flower Girl

Isabella is one of the most beautiful preschoolers on the planet. Sweet, spunky, and strong-willed like most indigos. Her mom, Maggie, brought her to me because Isabella began to have nightmares about her upcoming stint as a flower girl. She was scared to do it all alone at 4 years old, and that's totally understandable.

Working with Isabella, I helped her understand that fear simply means we've never done something before—that's it. That helped her. So along with coaching Isabella, I balanced her energy with Reiki and crystals, and also recommended the use of a flower essence on the day of the wedding.

Actually, Isabella said, "You mean I can eat flowers?" and of course, I explained how flower essences were made and that only certain flowers were edible. She asked her mom to pick up some flowers to eat (which you can) and also the flower remedy so that she could feel courageous and calm on the wedding day.

Maggie was thrilled to see Isabella's enthusiasm return and her fears reduce as she realized that being scared was okay. They both set off on an excursion to use flowers therapeutically and picked up the Bach Rescue Remedy for children, which Isabella thought was the coolest thing she has ever heard of.

Long story short, Isabella was a hit on the day of the wedding, and everyone commented about how she was the most beautiful flower girl they'd seen.

Flower Essences
"God is in the flowers."

—Noah, age 4

Working with the energy of flowers can be done in a number of wonderful ways. You can use fresh flowers, use flower essences, and even grow a flower garden (backyard or in pots). Flowers have auras and are living beings. With that understanding, it's always good to be grateful to flowers for giving of themselves to us.

Using flowers medicinally is equally effective for girls and boys. Some specific ways that you can begin healing with flowers include:

⊃ **Baths.** You can either use 15 to 20 drops of a flower essence in a bath for your indigo or flower petals. Energetically the flower essence will interact with their energy field and help them relax.

⊃ **Chakra balancing.** Similar to placing stones on or near the indigo energy centers, you can also use flower petals. It's the energy of the flower that can help restore balance in indigos electromagnetic field.

⊃ **Sprays.** I absolutely love sprays because they are easy and immediately shift the energy of spaces. I use sage sprays for clearing rooms and people as well as rose water spray (especially after an indigo meltdown). Heritage Store (*www.heritagestore.com*) makes a great rosewater spray that's readily available, too.

⊃ **Fresh flowers.** I love fresh flowers and always feel an energetic lift when they are around me. Indigo children are the same way, and feel a heart connection with the life force of flowers, too.

⊃ **Flower remedies.** You can learn how to make tinctures, or remedies from the essence of flowers, or purchase them. Bach

Flower Remedies are the most well-known brand for easing stress and anxiety, and helping with sleep. (They also have remedies for pets.)

Your indigo children can also use photos of flowers and connect with them. They can imagine being surrounded by the flowers they need. For example, I led a meditation for one of my indigo clients to be surrounded by sunflowers. She smiled immediately. Sunflowers are beautiful, and their essence lifts sadness. So in case you cannot get the exact flower or essence you need today, there's always a creative way to draw upon flowers.

Alternatively, I also love to drink tea and find jasmine leaves in my tea quite wonderful. Most Western indigo children don't necessarily drink tea early in life. However, if your family does enjoy tea together this can be another viable option. (Jasmine tea has small amounts of caffeine so be forewarned.) Jasmine tea is also associated with increased calmness similar to lavender.

Flowers by Chakra

Certain flowers can energetically shift children's emotions, calm them down, and soothe their upsets. Becoming creative with how you use the energy of

Energy Center	Color	Short Meaning	Flower	Helps With
Crown	White	Spiritual connection	Lotus, tulip, lily, wisteria, white rose, magnolia	Feeling peace, trust in universe
Third Eye	Indigo	Intuition	Geranium, jasmine, crocus, iris, lavender, pansy	Calming, intuition
Throat	Blue	Communication	Bird of paradise, daffodil, eucalyptus	Speaking up, clear boundaries, saying "no"
Heart	Green	Love, emotional balance	St. John's wort, sunflower, rose, Gerber daisy, calla lily, peony, Echinacea	Emotional balance
Solar Plexus	Yellow	Power	Lilac, lily, hibiscus, sunflower, marigold	Self-esteem, confidence
Sacral	Orange	Self-expression, creativity	Hydrangea, hyacinth, camellia, orchid	Self-trust
Root	Red	Survival, grounding	Daisy, carnation, Chrysanthemum	Grounding

NOTE: *All of these suggestions are based on my experience. The book* **Flower Therapy** *by Robert Reeves and Doreen Virtue also provides similar and further explanations.*

flowers can be enjoyable, too. You can place rose petals under their pillow, give them a lavender eye pillow, use certain flower essences (or essential oils) at their temples, or pick wildflowers together.

Along with intuitively connecting with flowers, you can also tune into the energy of the flowers and what energy center they can positively impact.

Connecting flower essences to energy centers is about the energy of the flowers. As you've probably already observed, the flowers at each chakra aren't necessarily the color of that chakra; the important connection is they hold the energy needed to balance (add or subtract) that energetic function.

One more flower essence, calendula, is commonly used to repair, protect, and strengthen the indigo auric field. One more caveat is to be careful and purchase essences that don't have alcohol content in them. Alcohol is used as a preservative (like in adult mouthwash) but isn't helpful for indigo children.

Indigo Cures

Specific energy that needs to be shifted with indigo children oftentimes deals with their intense emotions, heightened sensitivity, highly responsive nature, and challenges completing everyday tasks because they are focused on higher planes of consciousness.

Here are some common issues and flower essence remedies:

- ⊃ **Calming.** Use lavender at bedtime behind the ears or during their evening bath (15 to 20 drops). If you have fresh lavender, you can also place it in a bowl in their room as fragrance. One mom, Molly, got creative with her kids and put a little lavender on the soles of their feet, and it put them right to sleep.

- ⊃ **Reducing anxiety.** Lavender is again great to help children de-stress along with certain crystals that grid their room. Lilac, daffodils, jasmine, daisy, and tulips are also energetically infused with serenity. Bach Flower Remedies sells a Rescue Remedy for children (no alcohol in it) that helps them feel calmer, too.

- ⊃ **Focus.** Clematis is a flower essence to help adults and children focus. I personally find jasmine improves concentration and eases tension.

- ⊃ **Confidence.** Larch flower essence helps to boost confidence. Grapefruit (essential oil) is also a confidence booster.

⊃ **Anger release.** Red chestnut can help release fears and upsetting emotions like anger. Tiger lily, calendula, and snap dragon are helpful for soothing deep feelings of hostility. Roses will also open the heart.

⊃ **Grounding.** Daisy, carnation, clover, and chrysanthemum are helpful for children that need to feel more grounded.

Tapping into the tremendous healing power of flowers and learning about them with our indigo children connects us together. They feel seen, appreciated, and acknowledged as creative children with a keen interest in living closer to nature.

For additional reading, *Flower Therapy* by Doreen Virtue and Robert Reeves and *The Magic of Flowers* by Tess Whitehurst have further discussion about the use of flowers therapeutically.

Note: Flower essences are different than essential oils. Flower essences carry the energy of the flower and are made differently than essential oils. They are also water based, where oils are oil based. Oils can come from plants and trees, too, such as lemon, grapefruit, and eucalyptus (some of my favorites). Oils are stronger, too, so a little goes a long way.

Color Healing

"...color is energy—it actually has frequency, and these frequencies can affect our moods and even our performance."

—Meg Blackburn Losey

Color is medicine for indigo children. They can be calmed down by wearing or being surrounded by soothing colors, or vice versa. Every color has an energy signature, and when it comes into contact with our children they respond. In the same way that our indigo's energy field shifts when they are in close proximity to certain crystals or flower essences, the same phenomena occurs with the use of colors.

Using color to shift the energetics of our body isn't new. Ancient Egyptians used color, gemstones, and sunlight to cure illnesses. They realized that without the sun there could be no life. Seeing as our body is always moving toward self-healing the use of color and light is another way to facilitate that occurring.

Just recently, I found a *New York Times* article (July 6, 2012) sharing the modern use of color and light therapy helping with:

- ᗡ Premature babies (preventing jaundice in blue light).

- ⊃ Prisoners (calming them with pink rooms).

- ⊃ Skin conditions (ultraviolet light).

- ⊃ Reducing depression (sunlight lamp).

Scientifically speaking, the "minute amounts of electromagnetic energy that compose light affect one or more of the brain's neurotransmitters, chemicals that carry messages from nerve to nerve and nerve to muscle," as explained by Professor Harold Wohlforth, president of the German Academy of Color Sciences and photobiologist in a *New York Times* article. So the energy of light and color impact our electromagnetic field especially our sensitive indigos. Interestingly enough, Harold also has conducted studies by changing the colors of a school classroom from orange to blue, thus reducing children's systolic blood pressure (calming them down).

Somehow because we still haven't fully grasped the extent to which color and its highest vibration—light—can positively impact us, many people dismiss it. You may be one of those who think this is metaphysical "woo-woo" stuff for someone else. What I am asking is merely that you consider that light and color might have the power to positively shift your indigo's energy and emotional state, and help bring her back into balance.

Color Chart

Energy Center	Color	Temp	Meaning	Feeling Tone
Crown	White	Cool	Spiritual connection	Protection and angelic connection
Third Eye	Indigo	Cool	Intuition	Increases self-trust
Throat	Blue	Cool	Communication	Helps you speak up or say things
Heart	Green	Neutral	Peace, love	Soothes upsets, healing color
Solar Plexus	Yellow	Warm	Power	Helps kids focus and take tests
Sacral	Orange	Warm	Creativity	Lifts energy and spurs creativity
Root	Red	Warm	Security	Grounds children on Earth and gives strength

The Color Connection

"I cannot pretend to feel impartial about colors. I rejoice with the brilliant ones and am genuinely sorry for the poor browns."

—Winston Churchill

Organizing my closet by color came naturally to me. I tend to wear sea colors (teal, blue, coral, and green) and heart-centered ones (pink, greens). With these colors, I feel happier and more at home on this Planet. Our indigo children today are the same way. They literally digest the energy of the colors on or surrounding them, which influences their mood.

You've likely also felt the enormity of colors at one point. Say if you stood in front of a dramatic Florida sunset filled with purple and pinks? Or gone to the farmer's market and admired the array of colorful vegetables from pomegranates to peaches? Or perhaps decided to paint one of your rooms and stood amazed in front of the color samples at your hardware store?

Color is everywhere, and helping our indigo children use color to feel good regardless of what's happening in their lives is an energetic key to their happiness. Some of the ways to use color with our indigos include color swatches for chakra balancing, clothing colors, lighting, solarized water, room decorations, eating colorful foods, and flowers.

Color energy is absorbed through the skin, eyes, and auric field. So whether the color is light entering the eyes or swatches energetically getting absorbed into the electromagnetic field, the power is similar.

Other colors include pink as love (and also silliness, like bubble gum), silver as a deflecting color, especially around the aura, black helps with invisibility like Harry Potter's cloak of invisibility, and gold is another color of protection. Of course, there are more colors for your indigo children and you to explore, but this is a beginning.

Indigo Cures

Color changes the mood of a room, space, or person. In the world of color therapy, there are three basic colors: blues (cooling), green (neutral), and reds (warming). You can pick a color from these three basic color signatures to help your children cool down or to get them moving more.

Some basic color suggestions include:

⊃ Use cooling colors in the bedroom space (blues, purples, greens, lavender).

⊃ Use warming colors to "wake up."

⊃ Organize closets by color.

⊃   Select colors to help lift energy, focus, calm, or whatever is needed.

Similar to Daisy from Chapter 1, who only wanted to wear princess dresses, your indigo children likely have strong clothing preferences. They usually lean toward liking casual clothes, and everything must feel smooth on their skin—so no tight elastics on socks, tags on tops, itchy sweaters, or even stockings. Comfort is king for them.

But after you've done your best to offer them comfortable clothing, they likely have color preferences that say a lot about them. And if you need to balance or heal any energies, you can do it with their wardrobe, room decorations, lighting, and even using the colors of gemstones to bring more particular energies to them.

For more reading about energy and colors, Cyndi Dale discusses it in her book, *Energetic Boundaries.*

Blues Begone

Carey was feeling blue. He actually lost his furry friend, Buster, to bone cancer. Buster was a 14-year-old Labradoodle that was with Carey his whole 5-year-old life. Carey's mom, Vanessa, called me because Carey wouldn't stop crying and had a hard time with this loss.

One of the things I immediately suggested for Carey was to change the gray colors he was wearing, decorate his room differently (with more uplifting images and colors), and begin to shift the energy around him.

He was also scheduled to see me that week, but in the interim I wanted the heaviness around Carey to lift. So Vanessa came up with a creative project to honor Buster's life and also bring more color back into theirs. They had wanted to paint their playroom another color and thought maybe Carey painting scenes of the happy times with Buster on the walls would give him more peace, too.

And it was this color and creative therapy that Vanessa said "started bringing his love of life back again" and helped him realize that Buster isn't really gone. He's forever in his heart.

Sound Healing

"Sound, considered a mechanical wave, is able to penetrate the fields around us and produce near-instant effects in the body."

—Cyndi Dale

Sound is everywhere. It is one the most powerful forces in the universe. Oftentimes I wake up early to hear the sounds of the morning—from Tibetan monks chanting at sunrise when I lived in Asia to hearing the sounds of the waves crashing on the shore here in California. It is these sounds that strengthen, heal, and inspire me.

Using sound medicinally has occurred since the beginning of time. One of our earliest records is the aboriginal people of Australia using the didgeridoo, and also the Greek Philosopher Pythagorus recommending the use of the flute and lyre as healing instruments. So it needn't come as a surprise that sound healing has been used in nearly every ancient civilization and is also returning to popularity today.

Sound is energy work. It operates vibrationally, sending messages to our body, and our energy body responds immediately. You can probably recall a moment when you walked into a room playing beautiful music and—almost instantly—you felt better. It is this deep response that many of us have to music whether it's classical, contemporary, or hard rock. Our indigo children are the same way.

Our energy body operates on vibration, which gets translated into light, color, and sound. It is why when I work with indigos oftentimes I can see their energy. They'll also have blockages, and hands-on healing can bring them back into energetic balance. But there are times when you are at home with your indigos, and the easiest thing to do may be to change the acoustics of your surroundings to produce a better outcome (say more calmness, better communication, and greater harmony).

My suggestion is to think of sound as yet another energetic force to facilitate your children's healing and happiness. Of course, it is complementary medicine to be used alongside your main medical regimen.

Sounds Like...

Indigos intuit their lives and sound is a large part of that intelligence. Oftentimes I find indigo children with clairaudience (hearing guidance) to be particularly sensitive to the sounds in and around their lives. This often requires parents and other adults to carry noise-deafening headphones wherever they go. And that's a good thing!

So the question becomes: *What does sound healing look like for indigos?* Well, it can be used in a variety of ways. You can use classical music to help them relax, although I suggest Native American flute music (connected to sixth and seventh chakras). Studies also suggest that Tibetan Singing Bowls can change the brain waves and place people, especially sensitive children, into a deepened state of relaxation. In my experience, I can say that Tibetan Singing Bowls certainly help me feel calm no matter what.

Some other ways to use sound healing include:

- ⊃ Tuning forks.
- ⊃ Crystal bowls.
- ⊃ Chanting (or singing).

Claudia, a colleague of mine, has used tuning forks with her daughter since her birth. She became trained in a particular system called Acutonics, which integrates energy work (meridians, acupressure) along with tuning forks to achieve greater harmonic balance in children—especially our indigos. Joy, Claudia's daughter, is now 11 and frequently asks for tuning forks when problems arise.

For example, Joy's daughter tends to get headaches, and the purple tuning fork in their system is calibrated to the vibration of the upper chakra—thus by using it, it brings that chakra back into balance along with rest. By presenting the vibration of that chakra, it "resets" it and restores its natural energetic resonance.

Sound by Chakra

"For me, singing sad songs often has a way of healing a situation."

—Reba McEntire

Each energy center vibrates to a particular sound, and when it is matched then it can come back into balance quicker. Of course, this isn't a simple fix—but the use of sound can help indigos heal particular issues, feel calmer, focus better, and become their best selves.

In the chart on page 194, I share my own experience with how musical instruments connect to the indigo energy centers. One tidbit about me is that I listen to flute music as I write because it opens my crown chakra and connects me to higher wisdom. I also find the Native American flute particularly calming and centering.

Sound healers also believe that energy centers resonate with a particular musical key and that by using any instrument in that key an energy center comes into balance. Most sound healing books discuss this idea in greater detail.

What I have found most effective is helping indigo children release their excess energy through musical instruments such as drumming, and how it also simultaneously slows them down so they can relax. One of the great joys when I lived in Asheville, North Carolina, was participating in the community drum circle with other families. Jeremial, my friend's son, would look forward to Friday nights with such excitement to go into town, bring his snazzy drum, and join with others in feeling free to play whatever his heart desired. (Plus, he was exhausted after this, so everyone was happy and, yes, there was more harmony in the home.)

Energy Center	Color	Location	Musical Instrument
Crown	White	Above head	Flute
Third Eye	Indigo	Forehead	Tibetan Singing Bowls, Chanting *om*
Throat	Blue	Throat	Voice
Heart	Green	Chest	Drums
Solar Plexus	Yellow	Stomach	Piano
Sacral	Orange	Below belly button	Guitar
Root	Red	Tailbone	Rattles, Tambourines

Note: Use as a starting point for your sound healing repertoire.

Indigo Cures

As you well know, indigo children are all different, but including all of those unique quirks, they share common energetic tendencies. Some sound remedies to be used along with others include:

- ꙮ **Calmness and relaxation.** One way is to get them playing an instrument of their choosing, and this would be considered channeling their energy skillfully. Another way would be to play music that produces a calming effect such as Tibetan Singing Bowls, which have been evidenced to calm the brain.

- ꙮ **Improved focus.** Using headphones helps children focus better because they can eliminate all the distracting noise (cars passing by, television, chattering) so that is my first suggestion. My second suggestion is to primarily use music without words and get something that is both calming and clear, like music from Chopin or Mozart.

- ꙮ **Grounding.** Being able to play the drums is a very grounding exercise. Instruments made from Earth products like wooden rattles and gourd shakers, especially when used outside, help to ground, too. Raising indigos in the city or when inside, I suggest playing sounds of nature on headphones, and they can begin relaxing as well as grounding by hearing the ocean or birds chirping.

Being able to use music to soothe, strengthen, and empower your indigo children is energetic parenting at its best. One CD that I've been using recently is *Circle of the Soul* by Pamela Bruner, which incorporates the flute and harp. It is very soothing.

Indigo Healing

"Indigo children have access to human experience at a larger level, greater depth than most people do."

—Neale Donald Walsch

Shifting indigo children's energy through energy healing is vibrational medicine. It goes to the level of the cause and creates a wave of good vibrations (literally). Along with the energy healing methods that I have already mentioned, there are more ways to help recharge, renew, and restore our children back into balance. Some of them are:

Nature

Just yesterday, I was counseling parents about their son, Peter, who is a "different kid" on their farm in Santa Barbara. On the farm, Peter plays on the swings, enjoys his organic garden, and gets to watch the wildlife. He told me, "Moe, I love the deer. I am shy like them." At 4 years old he really feels calmer, more relaxed, and gentler in the serene setting of nature and being able to chill out.

Peter's mom, Margarita, has been working with him to feel calm in the city, but she feels it's not so easy. He hates being rushed, has become quite "defiant, throwing tantrums," in her words, and also sometimes just doesn't want to go to school. Working with Peter, it was easy to see how strongly he was an indigo child and also not only wanted, but needed nature to feel at home on this planet.

His favorite things to do so far are feeding the birds, watching the sunset, playing on the swings, petting the dog, working in the garden, and walking along the beach. With sunshine, wind in his hair, and the calmness of animals near him, Peter could connect to that place within him that feels calm and happy. So my work with Margarita was to teach Peter other ways to help him connect with that place when they are in the city (for example, deep breaths, visualization, prayer, listening to music).

Indigo Nature Benefits

⊃ Sunshine lifts mood (vitamin D benefit in moderation).

- ⊃ Grounding.
- ⊃ Energy release.
- ⊃ Calms anxiety.

Nutrition

Our indigos are exceptionally sensitive, which includes having peculiar (or particular) sensitivities to food, drinks, and supplements. Some of my indigo children have had dramatic responses to food dyes, tree nuts, brown rice, and chocolate. Although I am not a medical doctor, my experience has revealed that indigo children benefit greatly from:

- ⊃ Clean food.
- ⊃ Sugar-free diets.
- ⊃ Supplements.

By "clean" food I am not referring to the "regular" way of cleaning food but the concept of providing them food that is free of pesticides, preservatives, and other harmful chemicals that are often in foods. Of course, you need to make the best choices for your family; I am here to simply say that shifting toward healthier (more natural, alive) foods has dramatically shifted many of my child clients' energy, behavior, and moods.

One of my clients, Mathias, was 3 years old when his mom brought him to me. He was super sensitive but fierce in his energy. Mathias also had the "bad habit" of hitting his head when he was upset—and, of course, this wasn't okay. Understanding that all of our behavior has a biological basis, I suggested that his mom take Mathias to an ND (naturopathic doctor) to be tested for food sensitivities versus allergies. It was discovered that Mathias was very sensitive to gluten (a protein found in wheat and other grains), and when it was removed from his diet his mom said, "We've got a different kid."

I find many indigo children have food sensitivities, whether it's to dairy, eggs, nuts, or some other common grocery item. Discovering your kids' particular sensitivities is essential so you can replace them with better alternatives—things that don't give them headaches or rashes, cause fatigue, or make them hyperactive. One way to do that is to see a naturopathic doctor or through a simple elimination diet (temporarily remove possible allergen and see if behavior changes).

Eating is essential for all of us. But for indigos, they certainly feel the energy of whatever they eat and absorb it into their physical bodies. For this reason, whenever we can, I suggest giving them:

⊃ Organic foods (free from preservatives, food coloring, pesticides, and hormones).

➲ Protein shakes.

➲ Vitamin and mineral supplements.

Of course, there are other more obvious suggestions, too—like reducing or eliminating sugar and car-
bonation (toxins in beverages), and adding more fresh
vegetables and fruits. This isn't new news, but from
an energy perspective being mindful about the energy
of the foods, juices, and drinks we give children is a
key to their holistic health and healing.

Movement and More

> "Healing is movement. If you put the
> body in motion, you will change."
>
> —Gabrielle Roth

Getting energy moving again helps facilitate healing and unblocks stuck energies. It is the miracle of
movement, breathing, stretching, doing Yoga, and even
moving one's self to walk the dog that can provide an
opening. An opening for healing to take place, and
today to be the new beginning our indigo children need.

They need to begin again quite often like all of us.
So often they experience upsets whether they are physical, with stomachaches, or stress related, like anxiety
that they feel blocked. By getting their life force moving again and providing opportunities for stuck energy
to exit the body, then indigos feel better.

Some common ways that energy can move are:

⊃ Breathing exercises.

⊃ Stretches.

⊃ Yoga poses.

⊃ Sports.

⊃ Mindfulness walks.

⊃ Acupuncture and Tapping.

In Chapter 7, I share certain breathing exercises that are simple for young indigos to use anytime they need to let go of upsetting energies and emotions. It is in directing their breath that indigos can also create a sacred pause before acting out their impulsiveness, anger, and frustrations.

Along with breathing and physical movement, I have found Tapping and acupuncture to be great ways to get energy moving in the energy body. Tapping is non-invasive, and I provide some examples in Chapter 7, whereas acupuncture uses small needles that are hardly felt by most children. Of course, your indigos would need to be courageous for acupuncture, but it can be a viable way to unblock energies.

Coming Up

Our indigos are energetic beings. They get hurt deeply and wounds often occur at the energy body level, so using energy as a healer is very effective. I am also a proponent of holistic healthcare, which brings the very best of scientific and spiritual medicine together so that we can care for our sensitive children in a wholly, holy way.

Up next, I share with you how our indigos can be a success here on Planet Earth. Yes, it's possible, but as you are imagining they need to balance their natural talents with life skills so they can ground their genius here. I am not going to say it's always going to be easy, but I will say it's worth it.

Section III:
Success

Keys to Indigo
Success

Everyday Exercises

Keys *to* Indigo Success

"Just when the caterpillar thought the world was ending, he turned into a butterfly."

—Proverb

Seeing our indigos succeed is our deepest wish. Oftentimes the challenge comes because success means something different to each of us. I remember one conversation that I had with a father who told me: "My son, Charlie, is such a sweet and sensitive boy—I just don't understand what he'll do in the real world, though. We took him out of one school because the other boys were bullying him. Charlie didn't stand up for himself, or hit the other kids back. He just walks away and cries. I love this kid but I fear that he can't take care of himself."

Charlie's dad is a very outwardly successful man as the CEO of a Fortune 100 company and seemed so opposite Charlie. My role in helping him was really guiding him to see Charlie anew—learn his strengths, understand his energy, and get to believe that his son could be successful in this world. Because a big piece of this energetic parenting puzzle with indigos is learning how to help them be effective on Planet Earth.

Yes, it doesn't necessarily come naturally to indigos. They are operating from higher chakras and the lower ones are often closed. What this means in common lingo is they need to learn how to master life tasks, ground their energy, complete projects, manage their incredibly intense emotions better, and balance their constant need for creative play. Of course, I want them to have fun and enjoy life fully but also take full responsibility for themselves.

Conversations like the one I had with Charlie's dad are commonplace for me. Adults are always asking how they can help their indigos and highly sensitive children really persevere and find their place in the world. I wish there was an easy answer, but like Vince Lombardi is quoted as saying, "The only place where success comes before work is in the dictionary," and that is really true.

In this chapter, I am not going to give you more work to do, but really help you focus on making your current efforts highly effective. It is in the small, everyday things we do with our children where they learn how to master skills, complement their natural strengths, and move forward with confidence.

Seeing More Success

"For me, the most important thing in your life is to live your life with integrity and not to give into peer pressure, to try to be something you're not. To live your life as an honest and compassionate person. To contribute in some way."

—Ellen DeGeneres

Our indigo kids' energy resonates with what Ellen suggests: They are deeply committed to be who they came here to be, and that is likely different from anything that has come before them. It may challenge us as parents, teachers, counselors, and adults, but it is our work to help them find their way in this world. Of course, I would be lying if I said it was always easy or without struggle because that is not the way of life.

Life is here for us to learn, grow, and become more of ourselves. It is this indigo energy that can move us along the path of evolution. They aren't only little light bearers, but they so deeply need our counsel in creating a world that works for them.

When I hear parents ask me about how to help their children succeed, I often wonder if they are asking me: *How can my child make money someday? Can you guarantee my indigo's career path? What can I do to help them be stronger? Get better grades? Be less themselves and more like "regular" kids their age?*

Embracing our indigos as who they are, and also unconditionally loving them, is the start to helping them become successful. I've worked with countless parents and adults solely on seeing their kids differently. Instead of referring to them as challenging and difficult children, we can "flip the script" and see them anew. Shifting how we see them changes the situation from a crisis to an opportunity. This is where the miracle can happen.

When I work with indigos and their parents, step-parents, teachers, and others, I often see them succeed when they are fully supported. They feel the foundation under them and are more open to learn life skills that don't come naturally. Because let's face it: We are all not good at everything. We are not supposed to be. But we can learn and so can they.

Indigo Success

Indigo Success Model

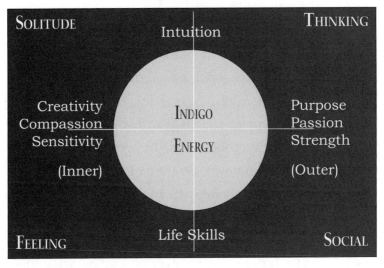

Indigo success model.

Our indigos came to succeed. They were born to share, shine, and glow. Whether you've got indigo boys or girls it doesn't matter. What does matter is that you are 100 percent committed to help them on their way.

Over and over again, I have found indigo children as a collective share not only a similar mindset but strengths, too. It is their intuition, compassion, sensitivity, moral compass, and creativity that come naturally. Said differently, they have an easier time connecting up (Source, Intuition) versus connecting down (Earth, task completion). As you so clearly know, they also need guidance on how to manage their energy and emotions, and make healthy friendships so that life works for them.

Indigos easily intuit life and navigate their world energetically. They have a natural time at the left side of the indigo success model, which deals with creativity, innovation, compassion, sensitivity, feelings, and private time. Indigos can come up with seven solutions to the Earth's energy problems all before noon but forget to write any of them down. So they need help to balance their natural creative side with the logical part of life— the part of their brain that can learn how to complete tasks, focus on projects, and bring ideas from the ethers down to earth. Indigos easily intuit life and navigate their world energetically. Five keys to indigo success follow.

Success Key: Balancing Intuition With Reason

One of the ways to help indigos develop this full brain thinking is to consciously raise them with right brain, left brain, and also full brain activities. Because they often tend to be so skewed toward the right brain, developing the left brain side in small steps will be helpful, as well as rewarding them for left brain successes like counting all the coins in their jars. Some specific brain activities are:

Right Brain	Drawing Painting Free-flow dancing Drumming Planting seeds Feeding the birds Writing a letter
Left Brain	Coloring in the lines Building with blocks Following directions Listening to music Designing a garden Hanging birdfeeders Mailing the letter
Whole Brain	Completing puzzles Practicing an instrument (while reading notes) Cooking with an adult Finding the address for the letter Reading a map Learning geography

Our aim is to help our indigos gain a sense of intuitive strength, balanced cognition, and the ability to access reason along with their creative mind.

Julius, one of my indigos, has gotten into a boatload of trouble because he doesn't always think before he speaks. Julius has a short fuse at 7 years old, and in school he told a child to "F" himself, and that landed him in the principal's office. Of course, I worked with Julius to channel his energy better but a big part of his success in second grade came when he began asking himself: *Will this get me in trouble? Do I want someone else to say this to me? Could I say this to my mom?* He began to reason with himself before speaking thus controlling his impulses or kneejerk reactions.

So helping children become inwardly strong, sensitive, and, yes, even reasonable when faced with challenges is a key to their success.

Success Key: Learning Life Skills

One of the biggest bugaboos that adults have with indigos is their lack of life skills. They are sometimes irresponsible, act independently (although ask you for money incessantly), and have difficulty finding their way, as Charlie's dad puts it, in the real world.

At the core of this challenge is their energy. They operate from higher chakras so easily staying connected to spirituality, intuition, creativity, and the cosmos. What they need help in is operating their lower chakras through grounding activities. One of my indigo clients keeps forgetting to eat, which is a very grounding exercise. His mom, Teresa, decided to help him remember eating by getting snazzy containers for his favorite healthy snacks (organic granola and Clif Bars for Kids) along with setting his watch alarm for two times a day to remind him to snack up for strength.

My suggestion is to focus on raising your indigos to learn how to be successful on Planet Earth and not assume school is taking care of that business. In most American schools, children are taught specific subjects (Math, English, Spanish, and History), but there isn't typically a time in the day where they focus on life skills like:

- ⊃ **Money management.** Indigos are brilliant minds but certainly need to learn how to operate on Planet Earth. Things that come easy to other people seem challenging to them. Like if they are given $10 for a week of school lunches, and they need to budget, this can go well or wrong very quickly. My recommendation is to begin teaching them early on about money (savings, spending, checkbooks, and credit); also, it forces you to get it "right" in your mind.

⊃ **Self-responsibility.** So many indigos are just given everything and are missing opportunities to learn how to take care of themselves. Okay, I admit they aren't going to get a paper route like I did when I was 12 (those days are long gone), but they can contribute to the family in setting the table, folding the clothes, or learning responsibility in other ways. One of my clients, Carly, at 7 years old decided to learn about recycling and be in charge of it for her house. She set up the green, blue, and paper bins. Bravo, Carly!

⊃ **The golden rule (ethics).** Indigos need to embrace the "golden rule," which says to treat others the way you want to be treated. Sensitive kids sometimes get caught up in the emotional moment and forget to be nice. So really reinforcing the idea of the golden rule, or karma in the East (law of cause and effect), is important to their character development.

Along with the golden rule, I want to also mention the "platinum rule," which says to treat yourself the way you want others to treat you. I first heard Michael Bernard Beckwith talk about this rule and how, ultimately, we are training others on how to treat us and I agree fully. So teaching both the golden and platinum rules are key to these children's life success.

One of my colleagues, Kris, has been teaching her daughter about self-responsibility. Her daughter, Anne, is 8 and gets a chance to make some money while contributing to household chores. She earns 50 cents any time she sets the table or takes out the trash; more intense chores are $1, like folding the clothes, feeding her younger brother, or watering the plants outside. (They've got a big garden.) One of the rewards is with her money earned she can spend it on anything she wants, like a new fish for her tank!

Success Key:
Seeing Sensitivity as a Strength

Seeing your children's sensitivity as a strength is essential. They can intuit answers, develop deep and genuine relationships, access higher dimensions of consciousness, and feel great compassion for others.

Albert Einstein said (according to the BBC's Website), "Logic will take you from A to B. Imagination will take you everywhere."

Being sensitive to your children can access their imagination, intuition, and innovativeness even to a deeper degree. Every great actor, artist, scientist, and scholar has gone beyond the regular level of sensitivity to be highly sensitive.

My first suggestion is really to see your children's sensitivity as an asset. Some adults have told me they see sensitivity as a handicap, weakness, or problem. And if you are one of those people, I implore you to consider seeing it differently. Although I realize both personally and professionally life can be challenging (at times) when you are sensitive, the benefits far outweigh the costs.

Some gifts of your sensitive indigos include:

⊃ **Intuition.** Indigos are exceedingly intuitive and can access their inner wisdom to navigate life situations. One of my indigo students, Erin, was able to take a math exam where she didn't know the answers, but she said to me, "Moe, I just guessed and got everything correct." It was her intuition at work.

つ **Creativity.** Indigo energy is exceptionally creative, innovative, and solution oriented, seeing things others don't. It is in their unique approach where they can solve problems whether they are at the personal, local, or global level. One of my indigo kids, Glenn, at age 6 organized how to hang the Christmas lights outside after his parents gave up thinking it wasn't going to work. Amazing, really.

つ **Giftedness.** Indigo children often have gifts in a certain area of life and don't necessarily fit into the regular model of schooling. So beginning to "see" your children's gifted nature without forcing them to be perfect is essential to their healthy development and nurturance of their talents. Jeff, a student of mine, at age 8 has already been in 20-plus television commercials although he's got dyslexia.

Along with these benefits of being sensitive, your indigo children need to learn how to balance their need for solitude with the worldly need of working with others. So much of the "good stuff" in life occurs when we co-create, collaborate, and partner with others to bring something into the world that's never been before.

Johnny Depp, an award-winning actor, has a great deal of indigo energy. His unique presentation, extraordinary talent, and deep sensitivity were his mark from an early age. Depp's mom gave him his first guitar at age 12, and he began learning how to healthfully channel his energy. Although he continues with his love of music, he took up acting at Nicolas Cage's suggestion and also learned to collaborate bringing to the big screen such characters like Captain Jack Sparrow.

So a key to indigo success is learning how to harness their intense energy and sensitivity to contribute something new to the world. This way it really can be an asset.

Success Key: Finding Their Purpose

Michael Bernard Beckwith, author and teacher, tells a story of how someone came up to him saying she found her inner porpoise. He politely smiled. She said, "I really meditated and found my inner porpoise like the guest speaker asked us too." Beckwith replied: "No, he was talking about your inner purpose," and they laughed.

Indigos excel when they find their purpose, whether it's working with porpoises or not. They feel like they fit in when they get to express their talents, share their gifts, and shine their Light. So many times indigos struggle on their way to their purpose because it's not something that they have heard of necessarily before.

Take me, for example. When I went to school I was taught by Catholic nuns up until eighth grade and then by the Jesuits. Although, I received excellent training in Christianity, there was never any discussion about becoming an author or energy healer. They were merely seeking to place us into one of the traditional square pegs: doctor, lawyer, teacher, nurse, professor, and so on. But I was a circular kid. Sometimes this still happens with today's indigos who don't fit into any models.

Indigos came to contribute in ways we can't even imagine. So it's best if we don't limit them by our way of thinking. One of the great things that Einstein explained was that solutions cannot be solved at the same level of thinking that created the problem. And here's where our indigos are different; they can meditate, access other dimensions, and then bring solutions into form.

Sasha DiGuilianis, a professional rock climber, became the first woman, at age 18, to climb "Pure Imagination" in Kentucky's Red River Gorge. Her mom said (in an Adidas Outdoor video), "From a very young child, Sasha always climbed. She climbed everything. Long before she could walk she climbed out of her crib." With a fierce determination to climb, indigo personality, and intense energy Sasha found a purpose for her energy.

Some practical tips to help indigos find their way include:

- ⊃ Sign them up for things of interest.
- ⊃ Observe their strengths.
- ⊃ Don't overschedule.
- ⊃ Encourage them.
- ⊃ Partner with them.
- ⊃ Be their biggest fan.
- ⊃ Table your own projections.
- ⊃ Be optimistic.
- ⊃ Allow them the space to change.
- ⊃ Share real-life success stories.

One of my indigos, Samuel, at 4 years old told me, "I want to be a rescue pilot," and I was impressed. What really got me intrigued was when he was so observant, and noticed that I had a Red Cross radio (operated by solar power) and said, "I am going to need that someday." Sometimes indigos know early on what they want to do, and other times they are called to enjoy the journey of discovering.

Our gifts can also emerge in different ways at different times. When I was a counselor in business I would like to think that was one step to where I am today. It wasn't a "wrong turn" but a lesson to learn. Same thing happens with our indigos. They might want to be a dancer today and a teacher tomorrow. Give them the space to learn, discover, and evolve how they channel their gifts.

Bono from the rock band U2 is considered to be an early indigo. His unique personality, high sensitivity, fierce determination to do things differently, and intense energy mark him as an early indigo. Bono's also gone from focusing solely on singing and songwriting to broadening his contributions and championing humanitarian causes such as the plight of many of the people in Africa. In other words, his purpose keeps expanding and evolving as he does—and this is so very indigo of him.

Success Key: Cultivating Social Skills

One "red thread" running through this book has been how to understand indigo energy and what you can do to help your children succeed. Besides teaching them ways to manage their energy and regulate their emotions something else exists: social skills.

Although I feel healthy proper etiquette is important for success in the world, I am not talking about where to put the spoon and knife. I am referring to the idea that indigo children tend to isolate themselves and prefer to play alone. And I have no problem with their tendency, although they also need to learn how to play well with others. My suggestion is to make sure they have:

- ⊃ **Indigo friends.** By befriending other indigos they feel more normalized and less alone in the world. They can also learn how to be a good friend, and this is an essential life skill that will serve them their whole lives.

- ⊃ **Opportunities to connect.** Ensuring that your indigos have play dates, after school programs of interest to them, or other ways to connect with other indigos is essential for them (for example, Boy Scouts or some common interest). Years ago when I ran my own children's art studio, so many of the kids in attendance became friends that I secretly thought that was my role—helping indigos make like-minded friends.

⊃ **Creative outlets.** I believe the best way for kids to make friends is through common interests whether it's soccer, singing, or something else. By joining together to be creative and also channel their energy they can have the added bonus of being social. I know Girl Scouts does that for many girls, and also helps them learn entrepreneurial skills like selling cookies.

Of course, they need to learn how to play with others without being "bossy," as one mom says her daughter, Audrey, is told she is. Or how to have healthy play dates with other sensitive children, whether it's at a water park or in the backyard. The importance of developing at least one good friend is life-changing.

Social skills can be learned, too. They are like a muscle that when exercised becomes stronger. I have found the following especially important for indigos to learn:

⊃ Making introductions.

⊃ Standing up tall.

⊃ Making eye contact.

⊃ Disagreeing calmly.

⊃ Telling someone no.

- Making real friends.
- Apologizing.
- Playing cooperatively.

One of my indigo kids, Kyle, was so shy that he never introduced himself. What we did together was a set of role-playing exercises. With each one he built his self-confidence and become more self-assured. We covered things like how to walk up to introduce one's self and also how to spot someone you might want to be friends with.

Core of Success

At the core of indigo children's success is helping them learn to manage their energy. They begin to identify their energy (feelings, thoughts) and channel it into constructive outlets, whether they are physical or mental. For example, an indigo who likes to read is just as skillful as one who is playing team sports like soccer or varsity badminton.

Along with energy management (specifically their mental, emotional, and spiritual energies) we need to guide them in the success keys of balancing:

- Intuition and reason.
- Thinking and feeling.
- Solitude and social time.

⊃   Timeless and time-based projects.

⊃   Inner and outer success skills.

So much of helping indigos succeed also has to do with tapping into their unique talents, cultivating their strengths, and building those skills. Anthony, age 11, was always a super smart and sensitive indigo who felt a bit too sensitive for this world. His father, a single parent, always did the best he could but sometimes still felt like he was failing with Anthony. One day at school they began having cooking classes and something inside of Antony "lit up"; he said from that moment he knew he wanted to be a chef.

Our indigos can succeed here, but the point is that they need our support even when it's hard and challenging. One thing I have learned is kids that feel like they are the hardest to love are the ones who need it the most. And this is definitely true with indigos!

Questions and Answers

"Quality questions create a quality life. Successful people ask better questions, and as a result, they get better answers."

—Tony Robbins

Whenever I attend a lecture, whether it's Marianne Williamson in Los Angeles or someone else, I get so much from the questions at the end of the evening. It seems if one person has the question, so many more do, too. In this section, I am sharing some of the recent questions related to helping our indigos succeed that I have received.

QUESTION: My daughter, Maple, is 4 years old and doesn't want to go to birthday parties. Do I force her?

ANSWER: I would not force Maple to attend parties. At 4 years old, she is still rather young and learning to navigate her feelings. What I would do is partner with her and ask some additional questions, like: *What about these birthday parties don't you like? Do you want to have a birthday party? If no, what would you rather do to celebrate when it's your birthday?* I would really listen, acknowledge her feelings, and help her feel validated. At the same time, I would also suggest helping Maple manage her energy, protect herself energetically (see Chapter 7), and channel her intensity into something productive, whether it's gardening, gymnastics, or something else.

QUESTION: My son, Gabe, is missing social cues. What do I do? I was thinking of getting him an occupational therapist to help him. He's 6 years old, by the way.

ANSWER: Your son, Gabe, is young and still learning how to handle his energy, emotions, and social situations. It would be helpful to learn what types of social cues he is missing. For example, was he missing reading his classmates and they don't want to play with him—but he just doesn't notice? Or it might be other cues like the teacher raising her voice and through her inflection becoming upset? Indigos need to learn early-on how to read social cues and, seeing as they process differently, they may not always pick up these social nuances naturally. So my recommendation is for you to work with him on "getting" these messages, and then see what type of progress he makes. Please report back to me. We can then evaluate if he's moving forward on building skills, or might need additional support like occupational therapy or testing.

QUESTION: My daughter, Ellen, cannot stop
            interrupting in preschool. How can I help
            her?

ANSWER: Indigo kids' energy moves so fast, which
            includes their emotions, thoughts, and
            responses. Ellen is so far beyond her
            preschool class I imagine she is bored.
            When indigos interrupt they are thinking
            so quickly it just pops out of their mouth.
            So one thing we need to do as adults,
            teachers, and healers is help them slow
            down a little (pause) and then wait until
            an appropriate time to ask their question.
            Typically, I teach children specific
            breathing exercises to calm and center
            them in those moments.

QUESTION: Nora, my daughter, cannot let things go.
            She is 5 years old and a boy in her class
            called her soccer kick lame. Nora has
            probably talked to me 20 times about it in
            the last week. What do I do?

ANSWER: Most indigo children have trouble
            letting things go. They are so sensitive
            to criticism and don't understand why
            others say mean things. Indigos also feel
            so deeply and when upset are confused

between how they see the situation—and how someone else does. For example, Nora thought her kick was great, so why would this other kid say it was lame?

What Nora needs to understand is that just because someone says something doesn't mean it's true. Her kick was great. The other kid in the class was probably feeling stinky that day and was just sharing his stinky feelings; it was no reflection on her. So ultimately, Nora needed guidance from you and could also benefit from energy healing sessions.

QUESTION: My daughter, Audrey, at age 3, gets in trouble for being bossy at school daily. Any suggestions?

ANSWER: Indigos are born leaders. They want to lead and run the show. They are born negotiators, problem-solvers, and innovators, and see things differently versus wanting to conform to established rules (classroom or home). So the goal is helping Audrey navigate her current preschool and get along with others while not "beating out" her leadership skills. Audrey will benefit from learning how to participate in cooperative play and team activities, and at home you can let her lead. Or maybe you can even talk to her teacher to reframe how she sees Audrey from "bossy" to "future leader" so it's decidedly more positive.

QUESTION: How can I help my daughter, Rose, at age 4 feel her sensitivities really are a good thing? She is acutely aware of taste, smells, and sounds. We do carry noise-canceling headphones wherever we go.

ANSWER: You are off to a great start. You are managing her sound preferences and helping normalize them. That's step one. Also, I would accentuate the positive side of her keen sense of smell and taste. For example, I would sign her up for a kids' cooking class so she could really "see" her heightened sensitivities as an advantage. So in this situation maybe she can smell the difference among rosemary, thyme, peppermint, and oregano better than anyone.

QUESTION: My son, Zach, at age 11 refuses to go to a counselor but he is definitely stressed out. He cries every morning when it's time to go to school and struggles in social situations. Do I force him to go see a counselor?

ANSWER: Oftentimes indigos despise traditional talk therapy. They are more apt to see someone for play or art therapy, energy work, acupuncture, sound healing, or something more metaphysical. Zach certainly does need assistance, especially an indigo mentor to help him navigate his emotions, learn ways to let go of his upset, and channel his intensity into something skillful. So my answer to you is that I wouldn't force a counselor on him, but I would partner with him for a solution. Ask him what he would be open to such as energy work, acupuncture, art therapy, or something creative to get his energy moving again and jump-start his healing.

Of course, there might also be a sport or physical activity that becomes therapeutic for him too. Be open to creative solutions along with finding him an indigo mentor so he can move forward with more ease.

QUESTION: My son, Mason, is 3 and a half years old and he hates the "Happy Birthday" song. He finds music with vocals distracting and asks me to turn off music if he feels sad. Is this normal?

ANSWER: Indigos are very sensitive to sound. They are often clairaudient (clear hearing) so they feel uncomfortable with noises that have lyrics because it disrupts their intuitive connection. And every indigo kid is different, so not liking the birthday song is a quirk; everyone has their different quirks, and it's just a matter of loving him and helping him navigate this noisy world. I have found many sound sensitive indigos love soft headphones (like Bose) and bring them with them everywhere.

QUESTION: I feel like my son, Rome, at age 11, is a different kid at school. They say he's so well behaved and at home I have a "little monster." What do you think?

ANSWER: Indigos can suppress their intense energy for only so long. At school, Rome is doing his best to fit in—to conform— and the nature of indigo children is nonconforming. So at home, he can "let it all out" and be himself, while at school he's trying to please his teacher, classmates, and everyone but himself.

Rome really needs to learn how to be himself at school and home. Of course, there are times when we have to follow rules and guidelines even if we think they are a pain, but we've got to learn how to navigate those situations.

Your situation is one that I hear repeatedly from parents and gets alleviated by indigo mentors. Rome will do well to have someone else help him learn how to be himself (sensitive, intense, talented, and different) despite the pressure to fit in at school. Different is good, and he needs to believe that for his optimum health.

QUESTION: Catherine is very impulsive and illogical even at 10 years old. She just wants to play her guitar and if I make her stop, Catherine gets really upset and will sometimes run away to the local playground. She says, "Life is unfair and no one understands me." How can I help her?

ANSWER: What I am hearing is your daughter
is musically gifted and really wants to
develop her talents. She puts in time,
enjoys playing, and gets annoyed when
interrupted. It sounds like she is very
indigo, intense, and sensitive with her
music. Of course, we want to validate
Catherine that she's talented and seen as
the musical genius she is, but she also
needs to help with other "life tasks" like
setting the table, taking out the trash, and
participating in family events like going to
Grandma's (for example).

Again, I think an indigo mentor would
be successful here along with someone
helping her see a wider perspective. At 10
years old, she's frustrated, and the guitar
sounds like a great channel for her energy
but she may need something else, too
(for example, jumping on a trampoline or
taking Yoga). This along with you helping
her see that life is not only one-sided
(creative) but Earth focused (life tasks),
too, is important.

QUESTION: My granddaughter is completely spoiled.
She is 8 but acts like the world is here
to serve her. How can I help her become

more responsible on the weekends when she stays with us on the farm?

ANSWER: You are smart for noticing that your granddaughter needs some life skills and to learn self-responsibility. The more indigos learn how to take care of themselves (operate lower chakras) the more powerful they become, and can actually ground their unique talents on this planet. You mentioned having a farm so I imagine there are lots of responsibilities, whether it's feeding the chickens, watering the vegetables, or milking the cows, so I would show her what it takes to run a farm, ask her to help you, and underscore the importance of responsibility with her.

QUESTION: My son, Guy, is a soccer star. He's got a wall of trophies in his room and proudly displays them. His younger sister, an indigo, is really talented at helping others—counseling, caring for animals, and collecting crystals. It seems Allyson struggles because her gifts are more inward. I see her wanting something on the outside or more visible to reveal her gifts. Do you have any suggestions for me?

ANSWER: What comes to mind is having Allyson create a "Dream Board" where she can make a collage or magnet board hanging up all her dreams. It's where she can proudly display photos of herself crystal mining, or visiting huge crystals. She can also have pictures (drawn, found, taken) of animals she would like to care for someday or that are in her life today. I can see her writing to someone she admires, too, and that person writing her back, where she hangs that letter on this board. Be creative and fun, and incorporate her gifts, strengths, and future dreams.

Of course, it's also good Feng Shui to have indigos put their favorite wishes and dreams around them. It gives them permission to *dream big* and look to accomplish those dreams. Our indigo kids are also highly sensitive to their environments, so keeping her space clutter free and full of her favorite colors will be important for her, too.

QUESTION: I feel like I have done everything wrong with my indigo. I yelled, screamed, spanked, and got frustrated easily. Now, I am feeling more like myself and fear that I have ruined my 5-year-old. Will my son be damaged forever?

ANSWER: Indigos have a great deal of energy and healing capability. If you connect your son to people that can help him manage his feelings, grow his talents, heal his hurts, and find channels for his energy, he can be more than fine. Although I may sound like a broken record, having someone mentor him would be incredibly helpful, especially as he lets go of any stored pain and moves into a place of healing and creating more self-love. I also recommend energy healing sessions for him, too.

QUESTION: My son is in third grade and tells me what will happen next, and it does. What is going on?

ANSWER: Your son is very intuitive and hasn't closed down his connection to all there is. He's not to be feared. Do you know his main intuitive channel? Hearing, feeling, seeing, and knowing are primary ones. If you know how he mainly gets information it will be helpful because you can gear how you speak (or connect) with him. For example, if your son is clairaudient then his audio senses are extra aware and he'll be very sensitive to sound his whole life.

Up Next

Our sensitive children can be successful throughout their lives with help from people like us teaching them these energetic keys to success. Of course, life is sometimes "trial and error" but if we keep pointing them in the right direction with wisdom and unconditional love, they are well positioned to be the best version of themselves.

Up next, I will share some actual exercises like guided visualizations, breathing techniques, energetic protection practices, and more to help your indigos. My suggestion is always to do what speaks to you, and perhaps use these as a starting point. Our aim over and over again is to help our indigos manage their energy so they can share their gifts, create genuine relationships, enjoy their lives, and take the best care of themselves possible for sweet success.

I also hope you might like one of these techniques for yourself, too, because I always think role modeling these breathing exercises, Yoga moves, or energy exercises is the greatest way for our kids to learn—but read them over, and do what you feel inspired to do.

Everyday Exercises

"Love one another and
help others to rise
to the higher levels,
simply by pouring out
love. Love is infectious,
and the greatest
healing energy."
—Sai Baba

When I first met Sam, she was 12 years old and her parents were separating. Dad was unemployed and I suspect depressed. Mom was over-employed and my observations were that she ran the house. Samantha was suffering from severe stomachaches, and with all of her absences from school she might have to repeat seventh grade. It was a stressful time.

So meeting Samantha, I was pleasantly surprised. She was smart, sassy, and intelligent. It was also clear that Sam didn't have clear energetic boundaries; she took on everyone's pain and internalized it. I asked her to explain her situation, and Sam said: "My parents are separating. They fight all the time. I feel terrible and want them to get back together. My dad has been out of work for 10 years. He used to work for the phone company and go up on the polls. Mom says he is a hoarder now. I just don't know what to do."

Sam was feeling powerless in her situation. She heard her parents fighting daily, and also was put in the middle of these arguments (really, not good). Interestingly enough, Sam was actually in the gifted program and skipped a grade—so the idea of being left behind really hurt her sense of self-esteem. So our work together was in reframing this situation for Sam and helping her create better energetic boundaries.

Specifically, I helped Sam get back on her "energetic feet" and see herself more clearly as the capable and smart person she is. I mentored her and encouraged her to "catch up" with her peers so she didn't have to repeat this grade. Sam was game and was able to do it easily when she applied herself.

In the process of seeing Sam, I gave her energy treatments weekly and also—probably most pivotally—helped her create a daily practice where she learned how to protect and direct her own energy for the highest good. Sam says she religiously did the energy protection exercises every morning, which were simple yet had profound results for her. She felt more empowered and stronger.

Within this chapter, I share some of those daily exercises that I taught Sam and offer you a smorgasbord of energy exercises to teach your indigos how to protect, clear, and strengthen their energies.

Daily Practice
"Successful people are simply those
with successful habits."
—Brian Tracy

What I know for sure is that doing something every day changes your brain and creates a difference in your life. So many people in the New Age world so casually say, "Do you have a daily practice?" They are asking if you mediate, pray, or do affirmations (or the like) daily because they know the power of everyday effort.

Parenting is certainly a daily practice. It changes as the school year and family dynamics evolve. Oftentimes, we are doing our best to wake up our babes, feed them, clothe them, and get them to school on time. So if we add anything to what feels like an already jam-packed day it better be easy, simple, and really worth it. Yes? Yes!

So it's for that reason that I am sharing within this chapter two sections. First, I share the simple but really helpful exercises. Second, I share the slightly more involved ideas, but if you've got time they are awesome. It's up to you. You are the adult nurturing your indigo children, and it's got to work for your life (home or classroom).

Some of the easier exercises are geared to helping your indigo children quickly clear, protect, and shield their personal energy fields (auras). Seeing as they are so sensitive they often absorb the energy of their friends, peers, and environments without even thinking twice. By helping them learn to shield their energy they also become more self-confident, inwardly strong, and capable to face their day.

Other practices that I suggest in this chapter include channel-opening exercises (Yoga, stretches, Tapping, and breathing), meditation, prayer, affirmations, and music. This chapter can really be used as a bouncing-off point for your creativity and for your indigos to create a practice of joyful energy management.

As Esther Hicks says, "Life is supposed to be fun," so please have fun while learning and teaching these new tools to your tots.

Energy Protection

"The aura is itself a protective atmosphere that surrounds and embraces you, filtering out many of the energies you encounter and drawing in others that you need."

—Donna Eden

Our indigos' personal energy fields or auras are highly sensitive. They can absorb everything that surrounds them or become more discerning with what they allow in. To help our kids learn how to strengthen their auras, let things in that are positive and uplifting while deflecting the negative energies they need to become real good at simple energy-protection exercises. I am sharing some of the easiest and most effective ones here.

Aura Zip

Aura Zip is something we teach our children to do in their minds, or together with us. One main energy line runs from your tailbone (first chakra) to your mouth (above fifth chakra). So the idea is to imagine your whole energy field clean and then zip it up from bottom to top. Many kids actually perform the zipper action as if they are zipping up their energy field coat, and that helps them feel protected.

— —

You can say to your indigo:

> *Today, we are going to learn the Aura Zip. First, we need to feel calm and take a few deep breaths. Let's say three breaths (in nose, out mouth). Let's count to three of them. Breath 1, Breath 2, and now Breath 3 feeling more centered. There is a main energy line running up our bodies from our hips to our mouth. But let's zip it up like an energy suit in front of us so we are safe and protected. Put your hands by your hips and zip up your invisible energy up to your mouth—also see this zipper closing your energy bubble around you and protecting your energy. You are safe and energetically protected so you don't need to take on anyone else's energy. Do this anytime.*

— —

Bubble Up

Teaching your indigos to see themselves surrounded by a protective bubble works wonders. They can say, "Bubble Up" or visually imagine themselves surrounded by a Bubble. You can also use specific colors such as:

> Blue—Feeling calm
>
> Purple and Gold—Divine protection
>
> White—Angel protection
>
> Pink or Green—Love

— —

You can say to your indigo:

Anytime you want to feel protected say, "Bubble Up" and imagine an immediate bubble of light surrounding you. It keeps you safe and secure. It also doesn't allow any negativity in and keeps you feeling happy and safe. You can also send bubbles of protection to anyone, anytime.

— —

Simple exercises like this can be super helpful for indigo kids. They actually serve many purposes, too. First, it helps them feel more in control of their energy. Second, they are learning they can direct their lives through thought. Third, indigos are actually protecting their energy from negative influences, and this is a lifelong success skill. One of my clients, Jennifer, has a whole family of indigos and she asks everyone to "zip up" before getting out of the car for school each day. Sometimes they giggle but mostly they are happy to get the energetic reminder.

Shielding

Simple energy-protection exercises can make a tremendous difference. I have found kids love the Aura Zip and Bubble. Along with those easy exercises, some indigo kids benefit from even doing a little more to shield their energy. Energy shielding occurs when you call in the "big guns" like Archangel Michael to shield your energy. They act like energetic bouncers, ensuring only positive comes in and deflecting the negative.

Indigos who benefit from this added level of energy protection are those who are either in challenging environments, or need to enter them. For example, one indigo I worked with named Ben had his older sister in the hospital. Ben would visit her with his folks but afterward felt upset and not like himself. So along with saying "Bubble Up," Ben called in Archangel Michael to shield him, and he never had the same unexplainable exhaustion after the hospital excursions like he did before.

Angel Assistance

Archangel Michael is a non-denominational angel that can help anyone of any belief system experience more energy protection. If for some reason you feel uncomfortable calling on him, you can also use the simple words of "Angel/Source/God/Spirit, please shield me and protect my energy." I know this works, too.

— —

You can say to your indigo:

Sometimes, we want to feel more protected so along with your energy bubble, just ask Archangel Michael to protect you. He is super tall and can be everywhere at the same time. Archangel Michael also loves everyone regardless of religion or what you think. Imagine him in front of you, in back of you, to your left, to your right. He is super strong and can make you feel strong and safe. Archangel Michael is also full of purple and gold light and carries a sword of protection that doesn't let anyone else's energy into yours. You can ask him to come anytime, or can just say, "Angels come to me" and they will instantly.

— —

Calling upon angels is a powerful part of raising many indigo children. Over and over, I found indigos very connected to the angelic realm. And my personal experience seeing and channeling angels has been going on for years—so I can only attest to the fact they are real and that when you call on them, they come.

Angels are also present across every spiritual tradition. They are in the Old and New Testaments of the Bible, Torah, and Koran, and discussed as dakinis in the Buddhist tradition. Of course, I have come across some indigo children who don't believe in God or angels, too. My experience is these kids are often the exception opposed to the rule. But whatever your belief system, angel therapy as taught by best-selling author Doreen Virtue can be a powerful part of raising, nurturing, and connecting your indigos to the angelic realm and also their energetic power. Other energy shields include music, plants, and flower essences.

Clearing

Sometimes our indigos will inadvertently pick up negative energy and get it stuck on them like glue. It comes from being around upsetting situations, people, crowded places, or general negativity toward them—possibly from a bully, mean friend, or angry teacher. Years ago, I remember being in first grade and coming home with migraines. Only looking back can I so clearly see that I was "picking up" on my teacher's sadness, as she was getting a divorce and being overly harsh to us.

If I had known of my teacher's negativity, I might have been able to take a break, wash my hands, and ask for divine assistance in clearing the negativity. Simple but effective. It's really the power of your indigos' mind that has the capability to clear them whenever they need it but especially in challenging moments.

Here I offer some simple clearing techniques and also highlight the value of the daily shower (or bath) as a powerful clearing ritual—especially if done mindfully.

Vacuum

You may be familiar with this easy technique to clear energy and cut cords. The idea is to use an energetic vacuum and remove all negative energies and then fill up with positivity.

— —

You can say to your indigo:

> *We are going to imagine cleaning the energy around you. Close your eyes and I will lead you. See an invisible vacuum, like something Harry Potter would use, and have it vacuum away all the energy that's not yours around you. You vacuum in front of you, behind you, above you, below you, and all around. Your energy is 150 percent clean now and full of only you.*

*You may have heard your ears pop, and
that was energy leaving. Now imagine the
bubble of energy around you very bright and
shiny and perfectly round. Close it up. You
can even imagine a zipper closing it up and
leaving you feeling safe, supported, and with
all happy energy. Feel free to do this in your
mind whenever you need it. Open your eyes
whenever you are ready.*

— —

Water

Water is one of the best ways to clear the energy
body. Indigos can use drinking water or washing their
hands to quickly remove negative energies. Another
option is blessing water, even a water fountain, and
when you drink from it imagine the water is clearing
your inner and outer system so you feel stronger. I am
sure you can find the words to describe or role model
this to your kids.

One other way to help indigos use water to clear
their energy field is to bless it during baths and show-
ers. (Yes, I realize sometimes it's hard to get them into
the shower or bath!)

— —

You can say to your indigo:

*Whenever you are in the bath or shower
imagine the water is washing away any*

*stinky feelings, upset, or anything else you
might have. You can then imagine in your
HAPPY energy that you say, "Bubble Up," and
you are safely protected. You can also do this
at school just by washing your hands and
asking it to wash away anything you don't
feel good about. It really works—I promise.*

— —

Of course, there are other, more involved ways to
also clear energy, too. Some of them are smudging
(using sage), chimes, carrying rose water, holding selenite, sitting in nature for 10 minutes, and being in
sunshine. I only say they are more involved because
your indigos may not instantly be able to do them
unless they carry a little rose water, or selenite in their
backpack—then I say do it. I especially like the selenite heart-shaped crystals because of how they feel
and the power within them.

Selenite Story

One first grade teacher, Mrs. Cooper, called me
because her classroom was out of control. She felt like
every day there was a meltdown, argument, or crying
episode, and the students were just not getting along.

So I decided to make a school visit and see what
she was talking about. Her classroom was bright red

(oh my goodness), had no natural sunlight or fresh air, and generally felt very claustrophobic versus opening. Mrs. Cooper agreed. So I made some suggestions that included:

- Fresh plants.
- Pet fish.
- Changing the room color (to yellow).
- Gridding the room with selenite.
- Creating a crystal learning corner.
- Implementing a peace corner.

Out of all these suggestions, Mrs. Cooper told me, "Maureen, I thought you were a little 'out there' when you suggested gridding the room with selenite—but it worked. The moment I used these crystals the room felt better and kids began to calm. Thank you again!"

Mrs. Cooper's progress was partly because she tackled her challenge from a number of fronts but very importantly was changing the energy of the classroom. It felt so dense and dark when I first visited there. With fresh plants and life, along with the crystals and a better room color, the energy was lifted. Indigo students subsequently felt an immediate improvement and there was less upset, too.

Channeling Energy
"Unused creativity isn't benign."
—Brene Brown

Every day children need to channel their energy, too. It may be something immediately available like breathing exercises or something more intricate like building a model airplane. The important point is that they do engage or immerse into something they enjoy every single day so they don't have any unused creativity.

Here I am going to share some simple breathing exercises that indigos can learn and do wherever they find themselves. The Hot Soup Breath is helpful to teach them to calm down and think before acting (that's usually a big one!) especially for young indigos. Breath of Fire is an activating breath when you need to get indigos moving again.

Breathing Exercises
The Hot Soup Breath

Most children know what it's like to blow on hot soup and cool it down. In this breath, I capitalize on that visualization so they can connect an invisible exercise to something very tangible for them. Of course, the gist is most kids have blown air out their mouth trying to cool down hot soup.

— —

You can say to your indigo:

> We are going to learn a new breathing
> exercise together. It helps us get calm quickly,
> feel better, and relax. Let's take air in our
> nose, and blow it out our mouth. Again, air
> in our nose and out our mouth like we are
> cooling hot soup. One more time: air in our
> nose, and out our mouth. Whenever we need
> to feel better take five Hot Soup Breaths and
> you'll feel calm instantly. Do them slowly and
> please remind me to do them too if I need
> them.

— —

Breath of Fire

Breath of Fire is a Yoga breath. It is when you take air in your nose and out your nose while feeling your belly move, thus calling it breath of fire. It is used when you need more energy and during energy clearing. Do not use this breath if your children need to calm down as it is activating and re-energizing.

— —

You can say to your indigo:

> Breath of Fire is to get our energy moving
> when we are sleepy but need to go to school,
> for example. Take air in your nose, keep

mouth closed, and blow air out your nose. If you have to open your mouth you can—but this is a Yoga breath that's usually done with air in the nose and out the nose, too. Again, let's take air in our nose and blow it out our nose. One more time. This time put your hand on your tummy so you can feel it the air moving. Air in your nose and then out your nose, feeling your tummy move too. You can do this a few times fast when you need to wake up.

— —

Breathing is a simple yet profound act. The mere act of directing our breath can bring us to a place of calmness. Be sure to do breathing exercises in moderation with your indigos because they are so sensitive to them—and if overdone, they can become ungrounded and spacey really quickly.

Breathing is one of many ways to channel energy. I emphasized it here because indigos are breathing all the time and when they learn to direct their breath—really use it—they can bring themselves to a place of peace, and everyone wins.

Bryan's Breakthrough

One of my little indigos, Bryan, at age 4 was getting in trouble all the time. He was hitting other kids in preschool, screaming at the teacher, and being very disruptive to the learning center, per his mom. What I noticed was that Bryan merely had so much energy that it needed a channel when he was upset and he didn't have one.

So I taught him The Hot Soup Breath, and he began doing it when he started to get angry. He needed it often at first. I also found out that some of the other preschoolers would "egg him on," which really got him angry.

The good news is that things really changed when he consistently did the breaths, and practiced at home with his mom. He even told me, "Thanks, Moe. When I do my breaths I feel better and don't want to hit anyone," and that really was the goal. By giving Bryan an alternative to swatting someone, he took it. He also learned those kids weren't his friends and began making some new ones.

Opening Channels

Energy that flows freely is the cause of health. Indigos who have healthy energy flow and skillful outlets, and learn how to harness their intense—angry, stubborn, and often defiant—energy can make genius contributions to the world. Yes, I realize parenting these little ones isn't for the weak of heart. But if you are reading this you can do it.

Some ways that you can help your indigos feel healthy and get their energy moving on an everyday basis include:

- Yoga poses.

- Tapping.

- Stretches (or walking).

By moving the physical body our energy moves. And this is why I love swimming regularly, hiking, and doing Yoga. Indigo kids are the same way. They need to move their energy since it is so intense and strong. To get you started, I am including a few Yoga poses and a Tapping exercise to jump start the energy flow.

Yoga

Yoga means "union," and is thus bringing together the body, mind, and spirit. It is also designed to get blocked energy moving again and produce a sense of calmness. Some Yoga poses that are helpful for indigos are:

Child's Pose. Kneeling on the ground, you place your head forward on the mat and your arms back. This is a pose to calm down the nervous system and relax.

Tree Pose.   Standing tall with your feet apart, you can place your arms on your hips. Then gently bring your right foot up and rest it on your left knee. So you are standing tall on one foot, the other foot resting gently on the knee, and if the feeling is stable you can then raise your arms upward like branches of a tree. (This is a good grounding exercise, too.)

Bow Pose.   Both hands are in front of you and then you make the movement as if you have a bow and arrow. Your left arm goes straight out to the left, and your right elbow is bent as if it is pulling an arrow back and moves toward the right. In this pose, your chest channels can open.

Yoga poses in the morning are a wonderful way to begin the day and start energy to move. Additional poses include Upward- and Downward-Facing Dog, Warrior Poses, Rag Doll, and more. One new book, *Yoga for Children* by Lisa Flynn, does a great job of sharing yoga poses beneficial for kids.

Tapping

Tapping was known previously as the Emotional Freedom Technique, and I suggest trying it. It works by gently tapping on certain acupressure points (for example, fleshy side of hand, eyebrows, side of eyes, under eyes, under nose, under chin, collarbone, and more). While you tap gently, you actually say a phrase that goes something like this:

*Even though I _____,
I deeply and completely love and accept
myself.*

So your indigo might have failed a test, and her saying might be:

*Even though I failed my math test, I
deeply and completely love and accept
myself.*

She does this while tapping specific acupressure points, and it begins getting stuck energy moving again. Of course, it is necessary to have someone (trained professional or parent) lead indigos in this process and when they are able (usually middle school) they can do it on their own when needed. Sayings may start like *"Even though I failed my Math Test, I deeply and completely love myself"* and then go toward *"I let all of this upset go and love myself right here."*

Currently, you can get a free e-book introduction at *www.thetappingsolution.com,* or look online for video exercises by experts like Nick Ortner, author of *The Tapping Solution.* I have taught Tapping to many indigo kids to release stuck energy and let go of upsets. One of my indigos, Seraphina, was in seventh grade and experienced a lot of emotional ups and downs. She told me, "Maureen, I use the Tapping when I am upset and it always makes me feel a little better."

The idea is to have our indigos moving their energy every day. Of course, it's because they need daily channels for their energy because, without them, it often comes out "wrong" in yelling, tantrums, and more. You can be as creative as you like; whether it's having them walk the dog or jump on the trampoline outside, there are countless ways for them to move their bodies and release that pent-up energy.

Energy Enhancers

"The good news is that we can engage in practices that get the energy moving in a healthy way and transform trapped energy into vibrant energy."

—Tess Whitehurst

Our indigos need to manage their energy. This isn't only for when they are acting out and have a surplus of energy. Everyday energy management is the crux of good health. Because it is the energy body that is within and around the physical body that, when taken care of, can help our indigos feel fantastic and stable.

Although some of these energy exercises take time, I promise they are time worth spending because the returns are extraordinary. Even as little as five minutes a day with your indigos sitting quietly, calming their mind, and slowing down can help give them a reference point for peace that they can return to throughout their lives. In other words, meditation can teach indigos how to stabilize their emotions and direct their energy.

Also, I want to be very clear. If formal meditation seems like "too much" to add to your daily routine right now, the important point is to begin incorporating meditative type experiences—so breathing exercises, Yoga poses, mindfulness walks, singing spiritual songs, or immersing in creative projects can be very meditative. Along with drawing upon wisdom teachings, getting an older indigo mentor and putting them into the right school system (that's a big one) they can move forward learning how to become more stable and enhance their energy systems in healthy ways.

Some of the energy-enhancing exercises that I recommend include regular meditation, affirmations, prayer, and incorporating music. Over the years, I have led children's meditations in spiritual centers, classrooms, and my private practice to help indigos learn how to find that place of peace easier. One of my tweens, Angie, told me it feels like "natural happy," and I would agree with her.

Meditation Exercises
Breathing

Breathing meditation is a form of one-pointed concentration where you simply focus on your breath. Indigos can learn to focus on breathing in and breathing out. With closed eyes in preferably a dimly lit room where they are sitting up in a straight back chair it usually works the best.

— —

You can say to your indigo:

Today, we are going to learn how to meditate. When you meditate you usually focus on one thing, and then become really relaxed. That's the goal. So we will close our eyes, and just focus on our breathing. Let's start. Closing our eyes, I'll guide us and then we will sit quietly. Our eyes are now closed and we can just feel our breathing naturally happen. We breathe in and we are thankful. We breathe out and feel calm. So let's just let our bodies naturally

*breathe and notice our breathing. If your
thoughts go other places just bring them back
to breathing and feeling calm. Let's do this for
five minutes today.*

(Set timer.)

— —

Chakra Clearing

Another type of meditation is visualization and that
you can do by leading your indigos step by step. In my
previous book, *Growing Happy Kids,* I shared a guided
visualization about how to help children meet their
Guardian Angels. In this meditation, we are going to
clear chakras and get healthy energy flowing.

— —

You can say to your indigo:

*In our bodies we have colors and lights that
are visible by certain people and certainly
angels. What I want us to do today is to
imagine cleaning our inner energy and
brightening us up to feel our very best.
So what I'll do is guide you to imagine
brightening up your inner colors, seeing them
the same size, and being open to feel happier.*

*We'll imagine certain colors from your
hips to your head getting shiny, brighter and*

*happier. Let's start with fire-engine **red** by
your hips. See it bright and shiny. Then, we
see **orange** like the color of fresh oranges
under your belly button. Wow, great job. We
move up to your tummy area and now see
bright **yellow** like the sun. It shines and
glows. Up now we go to your heart area and
see it as the brightest **green** we can imagine.
Going up even further, we go to our throat
area and see a bright **blue** color like the sky.
It feels so good. Now, we go to our eyebrows
and see a shiny indigo or **purple** color that
is bright like grapes. We love this color. And
above our head we see the whitest **white**
we've ever seen, and it's so bright it feels like
it comes from the heavens.*

*Our inner colors are now bright and happy.
Let's say, "Bubble Up" to close up our shiny
colors and keep us feeling upbeat all day long.
Open your eyes whenever you are ready.*

— —

Grounding

Grounding exercises can be really helpful to get
indigos centered on being here on Planet Earth. A
quick one is to get them naming things around them,
like Chair, Pillow, Lamp, Stuffed Toy, TV, and so on.

That focuses them on the here and now. Another way is also to help them visualize literally being rooted here and seeing roots from their feet into the center of the Earth—all imaginary, of course.

For example, Jimmy, one of my friend's sons, gets ungrounded quickly, and his mom says: "Do you have your roots today?" and if Jimmy says, "No," Mom asks him to see the roots from the soles of his feet going into the center of the Earth and staying grounded here all day.

Our aim in meditation is really to help indigos calm their minds and stabilize their energies. With time they'll learn they can harness their energy and direct it into anything they want. Of course, the real power is when indigos begin positively channeling their energy and using their intensity for some good cause.

Affirmations

Most people say affirmations from a place of disconnection, meaning they don't believe the affirmation and hence it has no power. Being able to say affirmations and believing them is everything. What that means is that before we teach indigos any affirmations we help them get into that place of connectedness so when they speak the words they are acted upon by the Universe.

Some great indigo affirmations to enhance energy are:

- ⊃ I love life.
- ⊃ Life loves me.
- ⊃ All is well.
- ⊃ I am safe.
- ⊃ I am awesome.
- ⊃ I am protected.
- ⊃ Angels surround me.
- ⊃ I am happy.
- ⊃ I am love.
- ⊃ I am having the best day ever!

Some of these affirmations were taken from Louise Hay and her extraordinary work on affirmations. Of course, they are only a starting point. The bottom line is that using affirmations with feeling and from a place of belief shifts our indigos energy. They are also learning how to talk to themselves in positive and uplifting ways, so please don't poo-poo this practice; it can be life-changing.

Shifting Energy

Oprah: *How do we best shift our energy?*

John of God (spiritual healer): *Love.*

Becoming really good teachers of love is our highest calling. It is helping our indigos choose love over fear that becomes part of our journey. In so many ways throughout their day indigos have to make choices; do they cheat on their exams like their peers, tell the truth to us even if they feel scared, or forgive their sister or brother? Learning how to choose love in the face of fear often takes practice.

Practicing to love is often done in the company of others. Actually, you can only learn how to love through relationships. It is for this reason that people come into our lives so we can deepen our experience of love, forgiveness, and compassion. And it is our indigos who are teaching us how to love more, and of course—in turn, we get to help them love themselves and the world in bigger ways.

Some ways to help teach our indigos to love and enhance their energy may be through:

- Prayer.
- Volunteer work.
- Donating/tithing.
- Self-care.

So many people around the globe have said that if we don't love ourselves we won't have anything left to give others. I can attest to that. I know firsthand that self-love is important—not from a place of ego, but from a place of appreciation that within you is the power and divinity to come forth and bring mighty gifts here. Our indigos need to learn that, too.

Loving is also not for wimps. Loving one's self and others takes a true spiritual warrior. Our indigos are born to birth new changes on this planet and bring an unconditional love to more people. This is why they struggle sometimes, too. They are encoded with this strong, fierce, and unrelenting type of love that wants to be born here and when they see things that feel so unloving they get upset.

Self-Healing

Being able to teach indigos energy work is awesome for me. Boys and girls leave my classes with a different perspective. They get to feel more empowered that they have the power within themselves to shift their energy.

Some of the benefits of having your indigo attuned to Reiki (energy healing) are:

- ⊃ Self-healing.
- ⊃ Stress relief.
- ⊃ Improved self-confidence.

⊃ Improved concentration.

⊃ Sense of empowerment.

⊃ Connection to their life path.

So many indigos are born as helpers and healers. They don't have tangible evidence of the inner healing arts, so helping them gain certifications, practice, and meet like-minded friends often gives them more concrete evidence.

Plus, I have seen indigos who are so sensitive suffer from test anxiety, social phobias, and depression improve dramatically by doing Reiki on themselves. One of my indigos, Casey, at age 7 has become the "go to" person on her block if anyone feels upset and she gives them an energy treatment—pets, too.

Indigo Parenting Prayer

Our indigos stretch us as parents. They help take away our hard edges and soften us as human beings. When we are connected to our indigos, we feel their love, intensity, and deep wish to make this world a better place. I can say there is no greater gift than being given the opportunity to nurture children.

Here is a short prayer that I created to center you and help you set intentions for raising and caring for your indigo children from a place of peace.

May I find peace within
And teach it to you.
May I find courage and faith
When troubles arise.
May I show you how to persevere
And overcome obstacles.
May you feel my love
Every day of your Life.
May I really see you
And celebrate you.
May we laugh a lot
And play together, too.
May I be a refuge for you
When storms come in.
May I be strong enough
To Let You Dream Your Dream.
May I forever
Respect and Honor You.
May I see Your Energy as Good
Intelligent, Powerful, and Light Filled.
May I feel Grateful for Our Time
And Trust it is Perfect
However Long or Short It is.
May you forgive me
When I make mistakes.
As our journey was destined
Our paths together
Lead us both home.

CONCLUSION:
Till We Meet Again

So many years ago, I would sit on my father's knee and he would sing "Happy Trails to You, Till We Meet Again" and I found it annoying. But with time, I have developed a real appreciation for the idea of meeting again. So instead of saying goodbye, I am genuinely going to say that I hope we meet again either in person or in the pages of a book.

Because I know we aren't done yet. We are just beginning the awesome journey of discovering how to help our new children grow up in a world that supports their success, strengthens their gifts, and grounds their genius in greater ways. One key to unlocking their best lives begins with energetically raising them—and that's what this book has been about.

So my wish for you is that this book is a new beginning—a fresh start that sets you on your perfect and right path of seeing these children energetically as well as guiding them to their greatness with more ease.

Bibliography

Aron, Elaine N. *The Highly Sensitive Child.* New York:
Broadway Books, 2002.

Bach, Edward, and E.J. Wheeler. *The Bach Flower
Remedies.* New York: McGraw Hill, 1998.

Beckwith, Michael Bernard. *Transcendence.* Culver
City, Calif.: Agape Media International, 2011.

Brennan, Barbara. *Hands of Light.* New York:
Bantam Books, 1988.

Bruce, Robert. *Energy Work.* Charlottesville, Va.:
Hamptons Roads Publishing Company, 2011.

Carroll, Lee, and Jan Tober. *The Indigo Children.*
Carlsbad, Calif.: Hay House, 1999.

Chiasson, Ann Marie. *Energy Healing.* Boulder, Colo.: Sounds True, 2013.

D'Angelo, James. T*he Healing Power of the Human Voice.* Rochester, Vt.: Healing Arts Press, 2005.

Dale, Cyndi. *Energetic Boundaries.* Boulder, Colo.: Sounds True, 2011.

———. *The Subtle Body.* Boulder, Colo.: Sounds True, 2009.

DiGiulian, Sasha. Video presented by Adidas Outdoor on December 3, 2011. Filmed and Edited by 3 SM. Found on youtube.com at *www.youtube.com/watch?v=rM9Btf-Ioos.*

Eden, Donna. *Energy Medicine.* New York: Tarcher, 1999.

———. *The Little Book of Energy Medicine.* New York: Tarcher, 2012.

Flynn, Linda. *Yoga for Children.* Avon, Mass.: Adams Media, 2013.

Foundation for Inner Peace. *A Course in Miracles.* Mill Valey, Calif.: Foundation for Inner Peace, 2007.

Gerber, Richard. *Vibrational Medicine.* Rochester, Vt.: Bear and Company, 2001.

Gienger, Michael. *Healing Crystals.* Scotland: Findhorn Press, 2005.

————. *The Healing Crystals First Aid Manual.*
Scotland: Findhorn Press, 2006.

Goldman, Jonathan. *The 7 Secrets of Sound Healing.*
Carlsbad, Calif.: Hay House: 2008.

Gruson, Lindsey. "Colors Has a Powerful Effect
on Behavior, Researchers Assert." *New
York Times,* July 6, 2012. *www.nytimes.
com/1982/10/19/science/color-has-a-
powerful-effect-on-behavior-researchers-
assert.html?pagewanted=all.*

Hall, Judy. *The Crystal Bible.* Cincinnati, Ohio:
Walking Stick Press, 2003.

————. *Crystal Prescriptions.* United Kingdom: John
Hunt Publishing, 2006.

————. *101 Power Crystals.* Minneapolis, Minn.: Fair
Winds Press, 2011.

Hay, Louise. *You Can Heal Your Life.* Carlsbad, Calif.:
Hay House, 1984.

Healy, Maureen. *Growing Happy Kids.* Deerfield
Beach, Fla.: HCI Books, 2012.

Hicks, Esther. *The Vortex.* Carlsbad, Calif.: Hay
House, 2009.

Indigo. Film produced and directed by Stephen
Simon. Monterey, Calif.: Monterey Video
Production (2005).

Indigo Evolution Documentary. Directed by Kent Romney and James Twyman. Los Angeles, Calif.: Emissary Productions, 2006.

Jaffe, Kabir, and Ritama Davidson. *Indigo Adults.* Franklin Lakes, N.J.: New Page Books, 2007.

Judith, Andodea. *Wheels of Light.* Woodbury, Minn.: Llewellyn Publications, 1987.

Keyes, Raven. *The Healing Power of Reiki.* Woodbury, Minn.: Llewellyn Publications, 2011.

Losey, Meg Blackburn. *The Children of the Now.* Franklin Lakes, N.J.: New Page Books, 2007.

Moon, Hibiscus. *Crystal Grids.* Self-published via CreateSpace, 2011.

Ortner, Nick. *The Tapping Solution.* Carlsbad, Calif.: Hay House, 2013.

Quest, Penelope. *Reiki for Life.* New York: Tarcher, 2010.

Rand, William Lee. *Reiki The Healing Touch.* Southfield, Mich.: Vision Publications, 1991.

Singer, Michael A. *The Untethered Soul.* Oakland, Calif.: New Harbinger Publications, 2007.

Stevens, Christine. *Music Medicine.* Boulder, Colo.: Sounds True, 2012.

Super Soul Sunday with Brene Brown, Oprah Winfrey Network, original air date March 17, 2013.

Super Soul Sunday with John of God, Oprah Winfrey Network, original air date March 17, 2013.

Tappe, Nancy, with Kathy Altaras. *Indigos*. Addison, Tex.: Aquila Media Productions, 2011.

Virtue, Doreen. *The Care and Feeding of Indigo Children*. Carlsbad, Calif.: Hay House, 2001.

———. *Indigo, Crystal and Rainbow Children* (audio). Carlsbad, Calif.: Hay House, 2005.

Virtue, Doreen, and Judith Lukomski. *Crystal Therapy*. Carlsbad, Calif.: Hay House, 2005.

Virtue, Doreen, and Robert Reeves. *Flower Therapy*. Carlsbad, Calif.: Hay House, 2012.

Weil, Andrew, and Kimba Arem. *Self-Healing With Sound and Music*. Boulder, Colo.: Sounds True, 2005.

Whitehurst, Tess. *The Good Energy Book*. Woodbury, Minn.: Llewellyn Publications, 2011.

———. *The Magic of Flowers*. Woodbury, Minn.: Llewellyn Publications, 2013.

Index

About *the* Author

MAUREEN DAWN HEALY is a spiritual teacher, energy healer, and counselor who works with parents and children globally. She specializes in indigo children and helping them succeed. Her last book, *Growing Happy Kids,* guided adults to nurture in their children a deeper sense of strength and ultimately happiness. Maureen's work has also been featured on Websites like Psychology Today and PBS, and across all media outlets such as Martha Stewart Living Radio and San Diego Living's Morning Show.

Unique about Maureen is her commitment to children globally. In 2007, she lived at the Base of the Himalayas and worked with Tibetan refugee children. Previously, she's been given recognition by Creative Visions Foundation and The Simha Foundation. Her traditional credentials also include a BA in psychology and an MBA from Clark University, and doctoral training in child development from Fielding and a Reiki Master Certification in the USUI lineage.

To learn more about Maureen's classes, sessions, and schedule, please visit *www.growinghappykids.com* or follow @mdhealy on Twitter.